Mr Shaha's RECIPES for WONDER

Adventures in Science Round the Kitchen Table

Alom Shaha & Emily Robertson

SCRIBBLE

I tried to fix it with superglue, but 'super' glue rarely lives up to its name. I resorted to taping the broken bits together, but it looked ugly and the blade wobbled when it spun. Frustrated, I smashed it on the ground. And there, among its entrails, I found something more exciting to play with.

How I became a Scientist

My mother once bought me a battery-operated helicopter from the local street market — a cheap plastic thing, bright yellow with flimsy white rotor blades that spun when a small red switch was flicked. It didn't actually fly, but to a young boy recently arrived in Britain from a Bangladeshi village with no electricity or running water, it was enchanting.

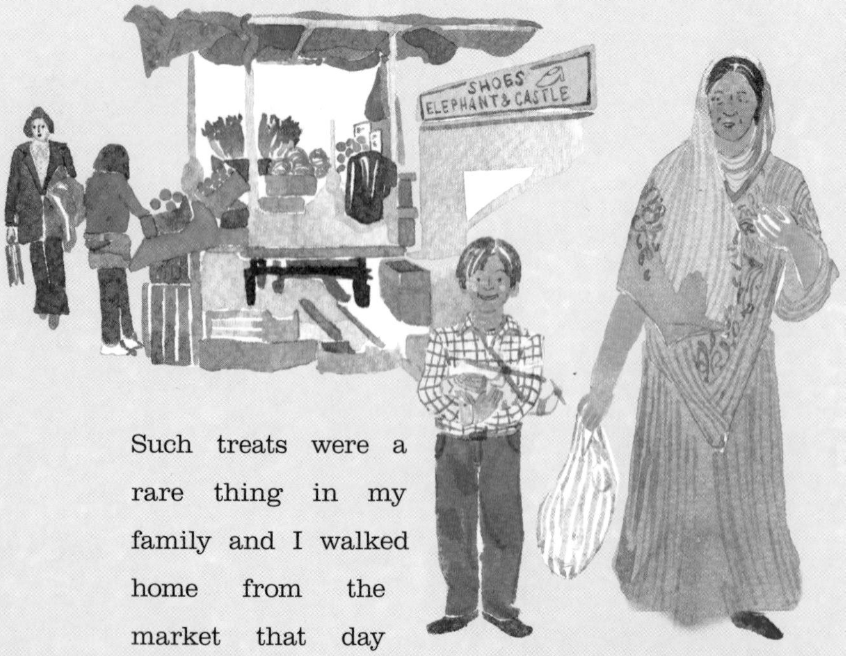
SHOES
ELEPHANT & CASTLE

Such treats were a rare thing in my family and I walked home from the market that day bursting with joy. But within minutes of taking the helicopter out of its box and playing with it, I snapped one of the rotor blades off in my hands.

The motor inside was a silver metal cylinder, flat on one end, with a spindle sticking out of the other. It had evidently been attached to the helicopter's blades via a number of plastic cogs. The most interesting thing to me was the simple circuitry that connected it to the batteries. I had discovered something that every schoolchild has to learn sooner or later: in order for a battery to power something electrical, you must have a complete circuit, an unbroken path for the current to travel from battery to device and back again.

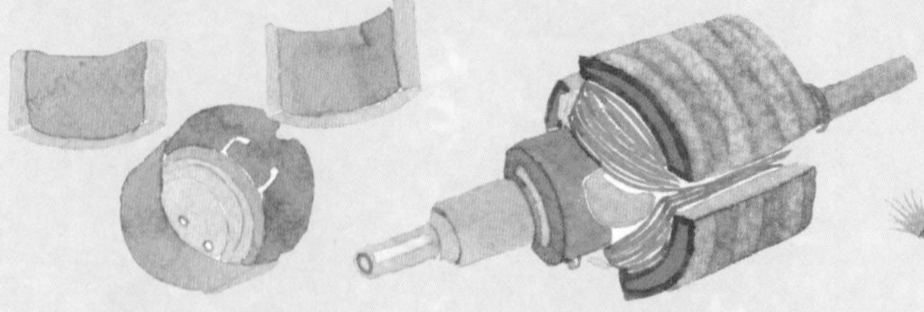

Dismantling the motor itself was harder work: it involved throwing it against a wall and prising open the case with a screwdriver. But the effort was worth it. Inside were two smooth curved parts that, much to my delight, turned out to be magnets. There was an odd-shaped piece of metal, around which was coiled incredibly thin, beautifully shiny, copper wire that did not stick to the magnets. But these innards revealed nothing about how the motor worked.

At this point, you might suspect that I've told you this story as a prelude to claiming that I was a naturally curious child who continued with these sorts of explorations, discovered some of the secrets of nature for myself, and grew up to become a brilliant scientist. But that's not how my story goes.

I was undoubtedly an inquisitive and playful boy who, like most children, looked at the natural world with wonder. But these things are not sufficient for a child to become a scientist or even to be able to look and think about the world scientifically. Any real scientific skills and knowledge I have is down to my science teachers, who trained me to look at, and think about, the world like a scientist. Not everyone is lucky enough to have such fine teachers.

Mr York
ON

It was Mr York, my physics teacher, who revealed the mystery of how an electric motor works. He connected a long, plastic-coated wire to both terminals of a power pack, then arranged the wire so that a length of it sat on top of a large, strong magnet. He showed that the wire did not stick to the magnet and that it was not electrically connected to it – so no electricity would flow between the wire and the magnet. Then he flicked the switch on the power supply, and the wire jumped into the air. I remember being astonished, as if I had just seen magic; I finally understood that an electric motor relies on the fact that a wire with an electric current in it becomes magnetic, and so can be made to move by a magnet.

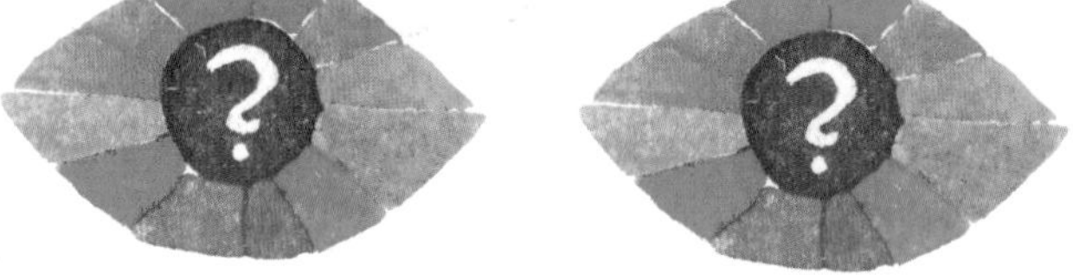

Mr York was using a powerful technique in science education – demonstration – to elicit joy, wonder, and, most importantly, curiosity from his students. As a science teacher myself, I love using entertaining, often spectacular, demonstrations to engage my students in what I believe is the first crucial step towards thinking and acting like a scientist: observation – looking more closely at the world than people ordinarily do. Follow that with enquiry – asking good questions – and experimentation, and that's it, you're doing science. When working with children, I summarise this as 'look, ask, play', and this book is filled with activities to help them do just that.

LOOK

I've chosen things that I believe will be fun to do, and I've also tried to include as many activities as possible that demand experimentation because that's a key part of what real scientists do.

ASK

It doesn't matter if you don't know any science yet. You soon will.

SCHOOL OF WONDER
add your pic here

How YOU can be a Scientist

You don't have to read this book from start to finish – just choose a 'recipe' you like the look of and start experimenting. I've tried to write my recipes in a manner that will equip you to start thinking like a scientist. Here's how they work:

• Each activity starts with something to **try out or build**. Follow the instructions and look closely at what happens. You might want to try to **predict** what will happen.

• Then start thinking about what's happened or is happening.

What will happen if we do something a bit different, and why?

(The table over the page has lots of ideas to get you started.)

• Try out **your own ideas,** too. You won't always know what will happen in your experiment – which is exactly why you should do it.

Notes and Records

Scientists record their results so they can prove that they've done the experiment, look back to see if there are any important patterns, and share their findings with others. Here are some ways you can record your results.

DAY 1
DAY 4
DAY 8
DAY 10
DAY 18
draw or photograph your discoveries
write notes
make a table of measurements

Safety first!

There are times when you will be working with fire and potentially toxic ingredients, so look out for this **warning symbol** in the instructions …

BE SAFE

There shouldn't be any danger to you as long as you are careful and sometimes get a grown-up to help. It's more fun to experiment with someone else anyway.

A note for grown-ups

If you're planning on doing an activity with a child or children, **read the whole experiment in advance** so that you are fully equipped to help them get the most out of it.

If you have the time, **try out the practical elements** of an activity on your own first, so that you can maximise its potential for eliciting wonder in children.

Most importantly, **make use of the suggested questions** in the book so that children are 'minds on' when doing the activity as well as 'hands on'.

Become a wondersmith!

Practice makes perfect.

Even if you have a gift for art or music or writing, you need to practise these things to become truly good at them. Similarly, children with a natural urge to understand how the world works need support to develop into scientists of any sort.

I've written this book to help parents, and other adults with children in their lives, to do this. These are my **'recipes for wonder'**, filled with ideas and instructions to turn anyone into a **wondersmith** – a grown-up who can foster wonder in both senses of the word, by encouraging children to feel **amazement** and admiration for the natural world, as well as to **ask questions** to learn more about it.

The power of 'I don't know'

It can be intimidating when someone asks a question you don't know the answer to, but I don't want it to hold you back from trying out science activities.

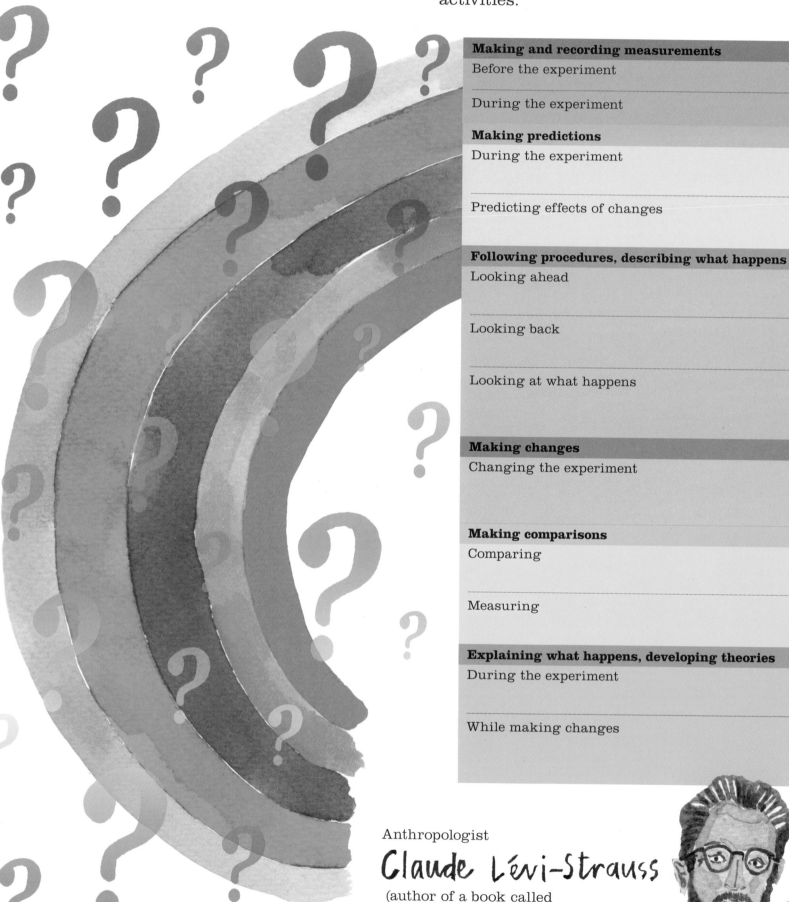

Making and recording measurements

Before the experiment

During the experiment

Making predictions

During the experiment

Predicting effects of changes

Following procedures, describing what happens

Looking ahead

Looking back

Looking at what happens

Making changes

Changing the experiment

Making comparisons

Comparing

Measuring

Explaining what happens, developing theories

During the experiment

While making changes

Anthropologist

Claude Lévi-Strauss

(author of a book called *The Raw and the Cooked*)

It's OK not to know the answers – the important thing is to go about finding them in a sensible way. I want you to embrace the power of **'I don't know'**.

There is a simple way to turn **'I don't know'** into a **positive** experience ... by adding the words **'how could we find out?'** The table here is designed to help you.

How can we measure what's going on?
How can we record our measurements?
What will happen next? What will happen when we add this?
What will happen if we make this longer/shorter? What will happen if we do this again?
What does the book say to do next? What can we do with this?
What did we do first? Next? Have we done this bit?
What happened when we did this? What did you see? Was that a surprise?
How could we make this bigger? Longer? Heavier? Faster? What else could we change? Are we doing a 'fair test'? (Are we only changing one thing at a time?)
Which is bigger? Longer? Heavier? Faster? Which took longest? Which was loudest?
How much longer is this? How long did it take?
What makes this move? Why doesn't this one sink?
Why do you say this one will fall faster? What will make this one get bigger? What makes you think that?

Scientists aren't people who give the right answers but ask the right questions.

CONTENTS

MOTION

Everything is moving, all the time. Even when you're standing still, blood moves through your arteries and veins, gases diffuse in and out of your cells, and the individual atoms of which you are made constantly vibrate.

The Earth upon which you stand spins upon its axis and races through space to complete its yearly orbit of the sun. Distant stars move away from us, while their light whizzes towards us. Stillness is impossible. Movement defines existence.

The scientific models and theories that inform our understanding of things (such as why apples fall from trees and why ice melts when heated) all rely on our ability to describe and explain the motion of things scientifically. From the celestial dance of galaxies to the microscopic jiggling of molecules, understanding how and why things move is central to science.

The activities in this section of the book have been chosen to give you an opportunity to explore, and perhaps discover, some of the key scientific ideas about motion for yourself.

CRISP-TIN CATAPULT

It's somehow more enjoyable to fire something from a catapult than to just throw it. A good one will let you launch something with more speed and precision than you could on your own.

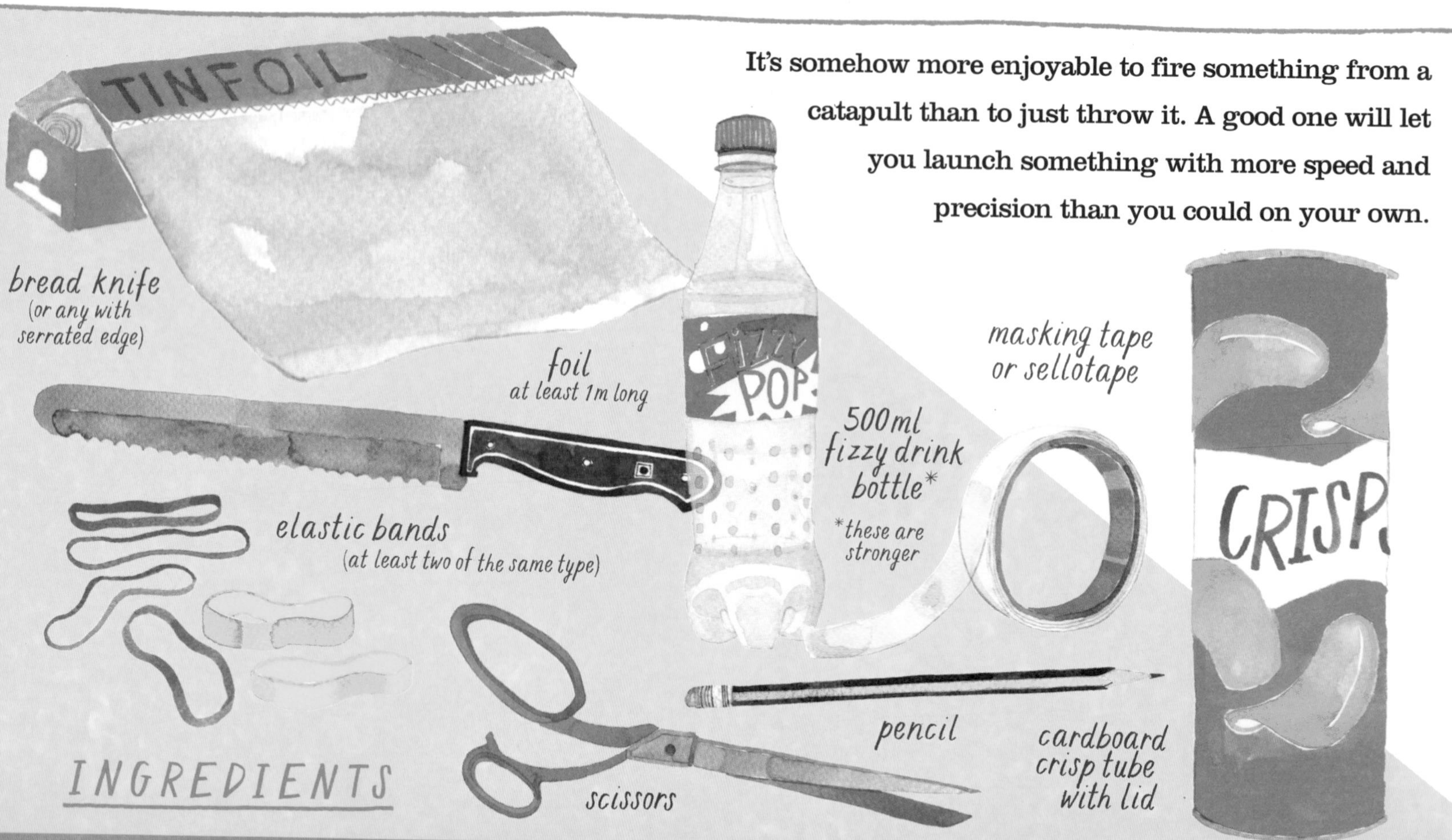

TINFOIL
bread knife
(or any with serrated edge)
foil
at least 1m long
FIZZY POP
500ml fizzy drink bottle*
*these are stronger
masking tape or sellotape
CRISPS
elastic bands
(at least two of the same type)
pencil
scissors
cardboard crisp tube with lid
INGREDIENTS

METHOD

! **1** Cut off the bottom of the tube. I find using a bread knife makes this quick and easy.

2 Cut two slits, about 2 cm long and 1 cm apart from each other, down from the open end of the tube. Repeat on the opposite side, as shown. This will form two tabs.

3 Slip a rubber band over each tab.

4 Use tape to secure the rubber bands. It's best to wrap the tape around at least twice to ensure they stay in place.

! **5** Carefully using the sharp point of a scissor blade, poke a pencil-sized hole on either side of the bottle 1/3 of the way down, as shown.

6 Push the pencil through the holes so that it sticks out evenly either side.

7 Now put the wide end of the bottle into the tube and pull each rubber band over the ends of the pencil.

turn the page »

2

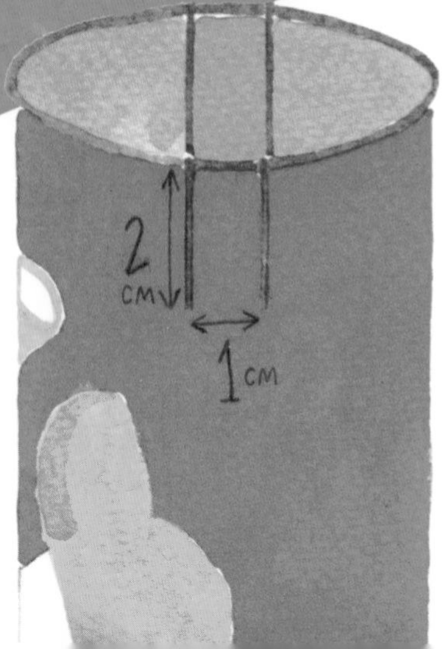

2 CM
1 CM

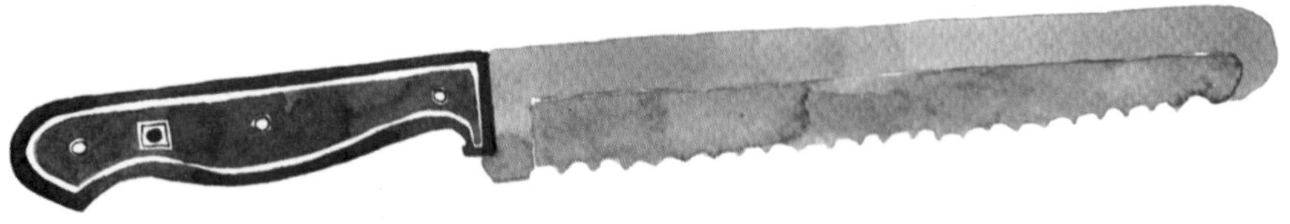

tape

4

5

BE SAFE

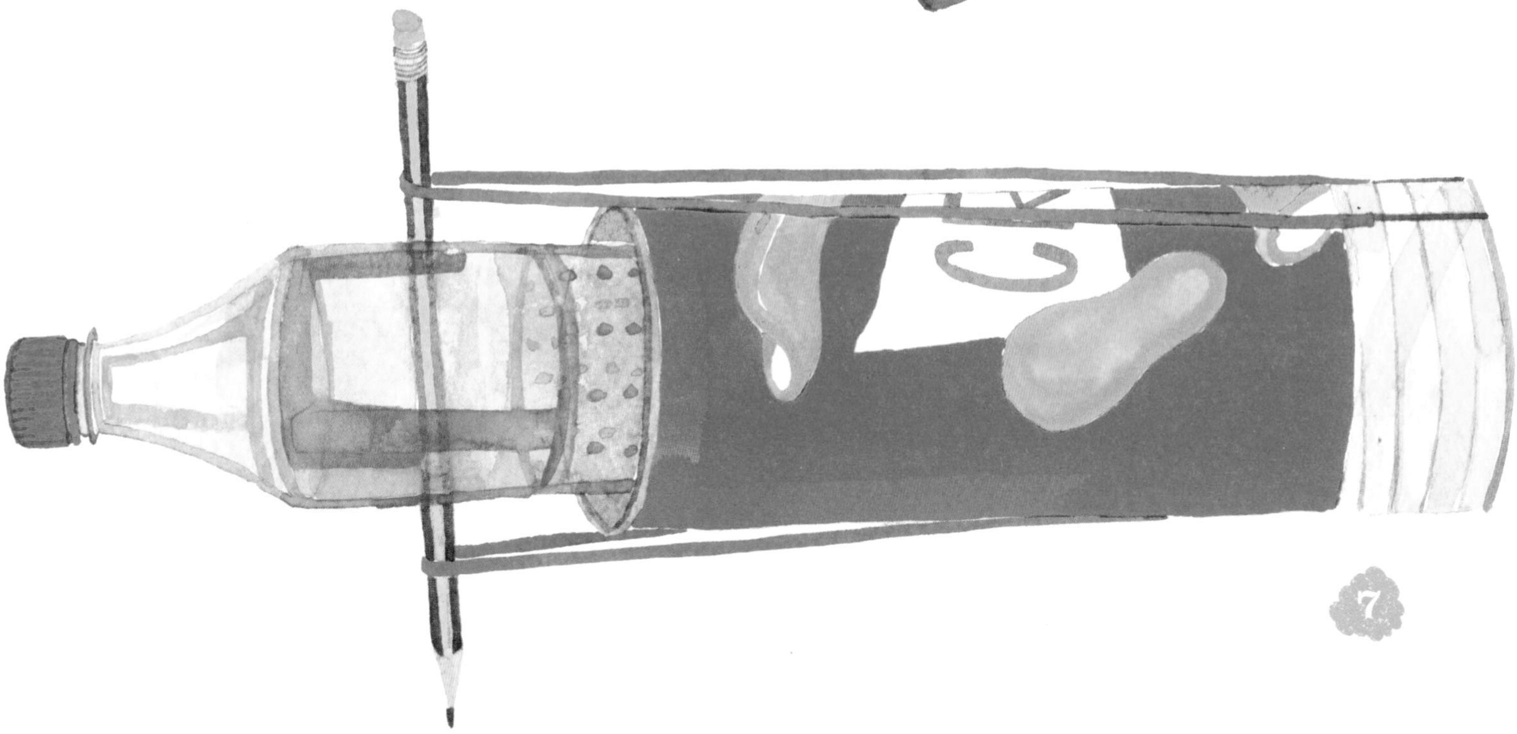

7

8 Scrunch the foil into a ball and put it into the end of the catapult.

9 Pull back the bottle and fire the ball!

You could try to hit a particular target, launch your ball into a basket, or use it to knock something down.

8

Try changing the **angle** at which you fire your catapult and see if that affects how far the ball goes.

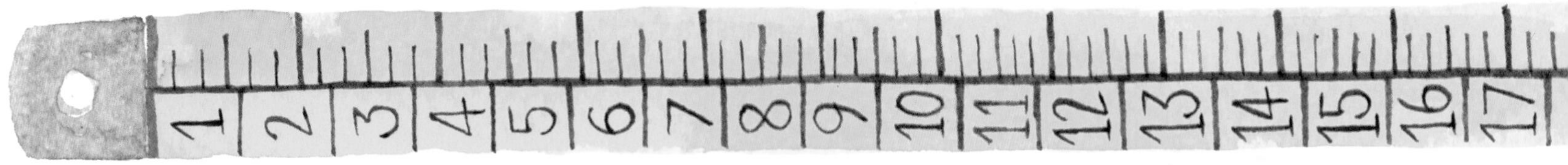
1
2
3
4
5
6
7
8
9
10
11
12
13
14
15
16
17

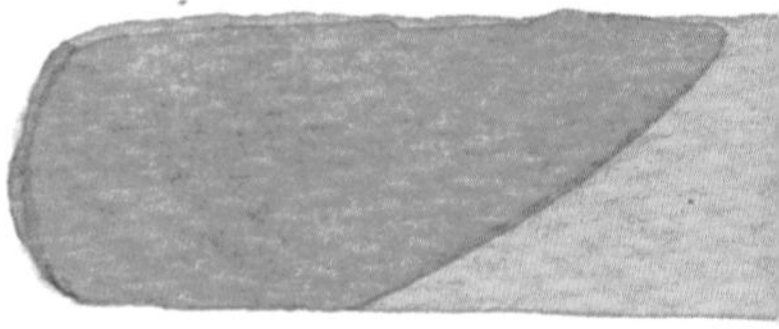

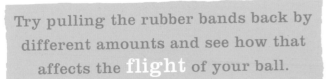

Try pulling the rubber bands back by different amounts and see how that affects the **flight** of your ball.

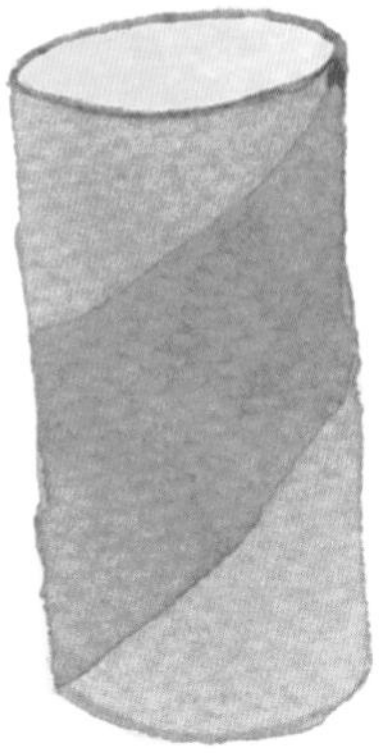

Try using different rubber bands, adding **more** rubber bands or changing the basic catapult design in other ways.

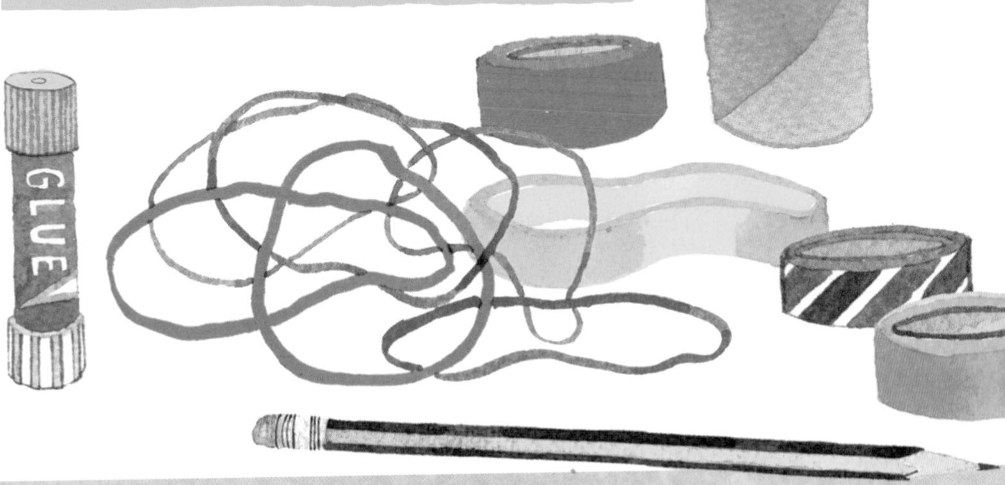
GLUE

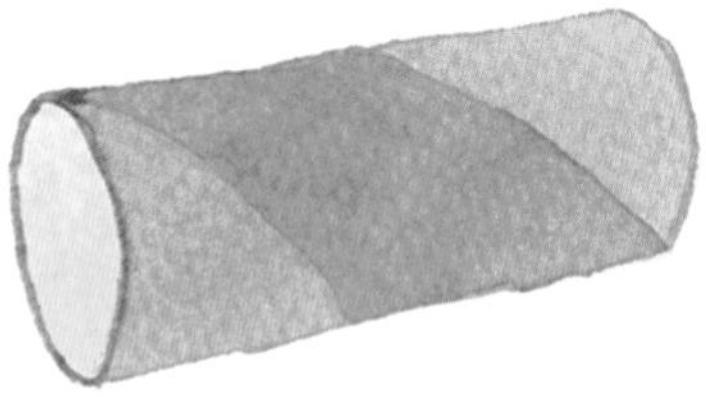

MR SHAHA says...

A good catapult will fire things much further than you could throw them because it allows you to give more energy to the projectile (a projectile is any object fired through the air). A crisp tube catapult stores energy when you stretch the rubber band, then transfers it quickly to the projectile when you let go.

Perhaps the more energy you give a projectile, the further it will travel? Try it and see! The distance a projectile travels depends on its mass, the amount of energy it's given (and so the speed at which it leaves the catapult) and the angle at which it's launched. It also depends on the strength of gravity – so you could try your catapult the next time you go to the Moon!

FIZZ ROCKETS

500ml drink bottle with sports cap lid
(that pops open)
mug/glass/jar
(that fits the upside-down bottle with its lid touching the bottom)
Fizzy VITAMIN
lukewarm water from the tap
fizzy vitamin tablets

INGREDIENTS

We say 'It's not rocket science', when trying to say something is not difficult. The basic science of how rockets work isn't really that complicated. But getting rockets to work is quite hard, and the history of science is full of stories of failed attempts to launch them. The rockets in this activity are tricky to get right, but provide a real thrill when they work.

? What do you think will happen if we put some tablets and water in a bottle and **close** the lid? Why?

SHUT!
1
4
SHAKE
4

METHOD

1 Take the lid off the bottle and make sure the cap is closed tight.

2 Half-fill the bottle with warm water.

3 Break two fizzy tablets in half and drop them into the bottle. (Watch what happens!)

4 Quickly screw the lid back on, give the bottle a shake and place it upside down in the mug/glass/jar.

! Stand back at least 2 m from the rocket, and wait.

5 If you find the bottle lid pops too soon, try using slightly colder water or half a tablet. Or if, after 3 minutes, it has not launched, try slightly warmer water. Experiment to find the best temperature. You may find that your rocket does not work the first time, but persevere because it can be spectacular.

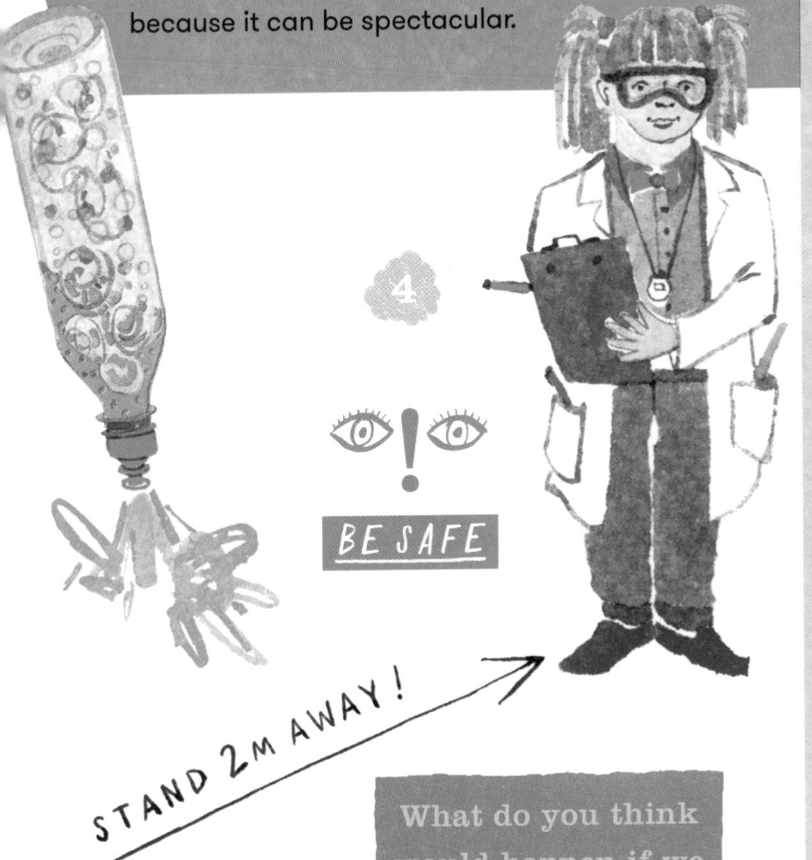

4
BE SAFE
STAND 2M AWAY!

What do you think would happen if we used **more** than one tablet? Why?

H2O

Perhaps investigate how the **temperature** of the water affects the reaction?

H2O

What things could we change to make the rocket go **higher?**

MR SHAHA says...

Fizzy vitamin tablets contain chemicals that react with water to make carbon dioxide gas. This builds up inside the bottle until the pressure is enough to pop the lid. When the lid pops, it pushes down on the bottom of the glass, propelling it up. Once in the air, the liquid coming out of the bottle pushes it along just as a real rocket's gases force it upwards. To learn more about this, try the next activity.

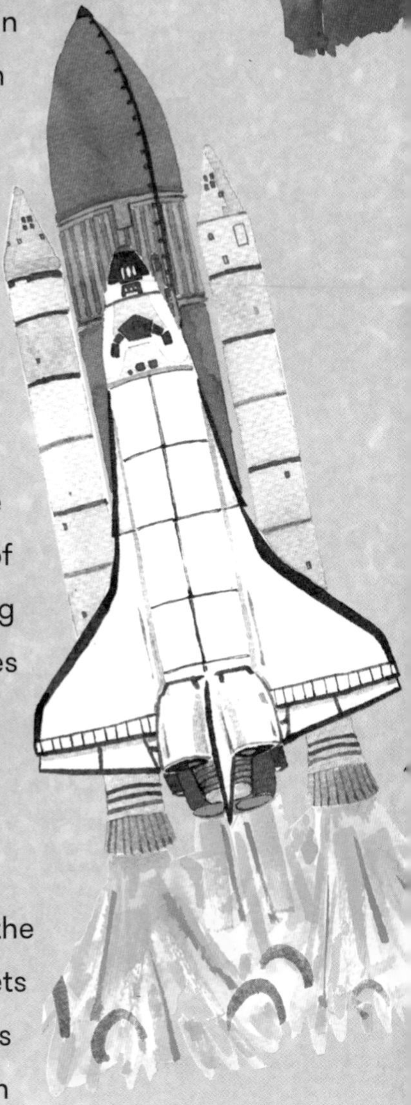

The hotter the water, the more vigorously the tablets produce a gas. This is because, in hot water, both the chemical particles from the tablet and the water molecules have more energy and move faster. So, they collide more often, producing more chemical reactions.

ENERGY!
ENERGY!
ENERGY!
ENERGY!

BALLOON-POWERED CARS

Have you ever blown up a balloon and let it go? Did it whizz around the room making a farting noise? You'll know that flying balloons seem to have a will of their own and zigzag around everywhere.

This activity is for anyone who has wanted to make the balloon go where they wanted it to. Let's build a balloon-powered car!

INGREDIENTS

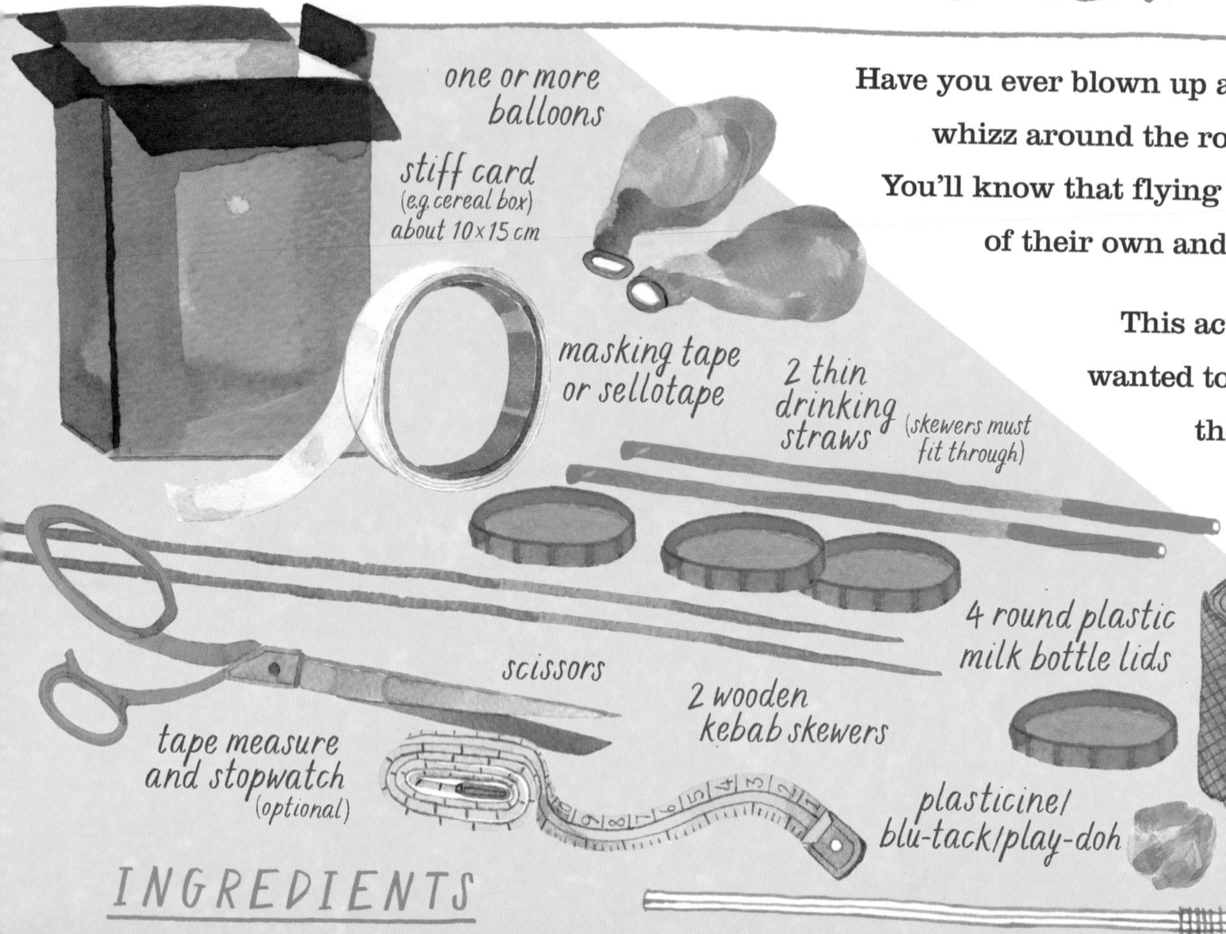

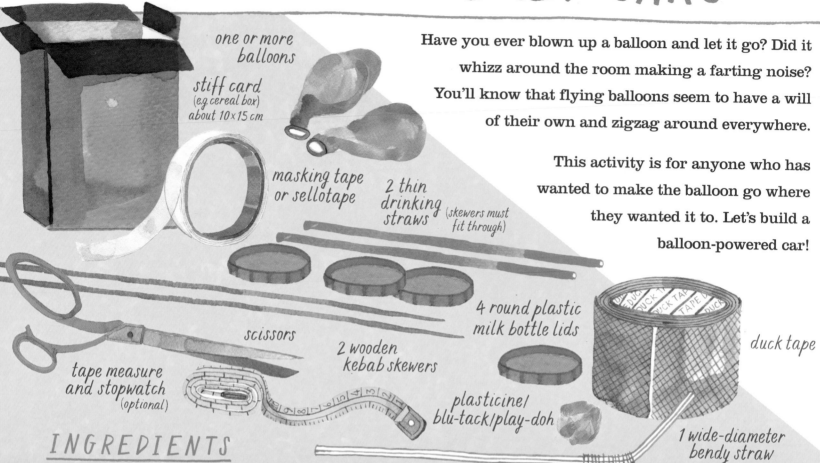

one or more balloons
stiff card (e.g. cereal box) about 10 × 15 cm
masking tape or sellotape
2 thin drinking straws (skewers must fit through)
scissors
2 wooden kebab skewers
4 round plastic milk bottle lids
tape measure and stopwatch (optional)
plasticine/ blu-tack/play-doh

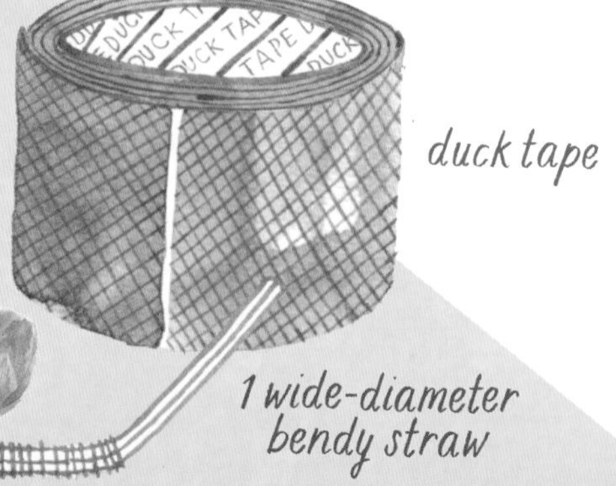

duck tape
1 wide-diameter bendy straw

METHOD

1 Tape two straws to one side of the card.

! **2** Place a bottle lid on top of a lump of plasticine or blu-tack and pierce it using a kebab skewer. Repeat this for each bottle lid.

! **3** Pass skewers through the straws and fix wheels on the end.

4 Turn the card over and tape a bendy straw in position. Tape the mouth of the balloon to the short end of the straw.

5 Blow into the straw to blow up your balloon. Don't let the air escape yet by placing a finger over the end of the straw.

6 Put your car on the floor.

7 Release the end of the straw and see what happens!

2
blu-tack

? Which direction should you point the straw in to make your car go **forward?**

! BE SAFE

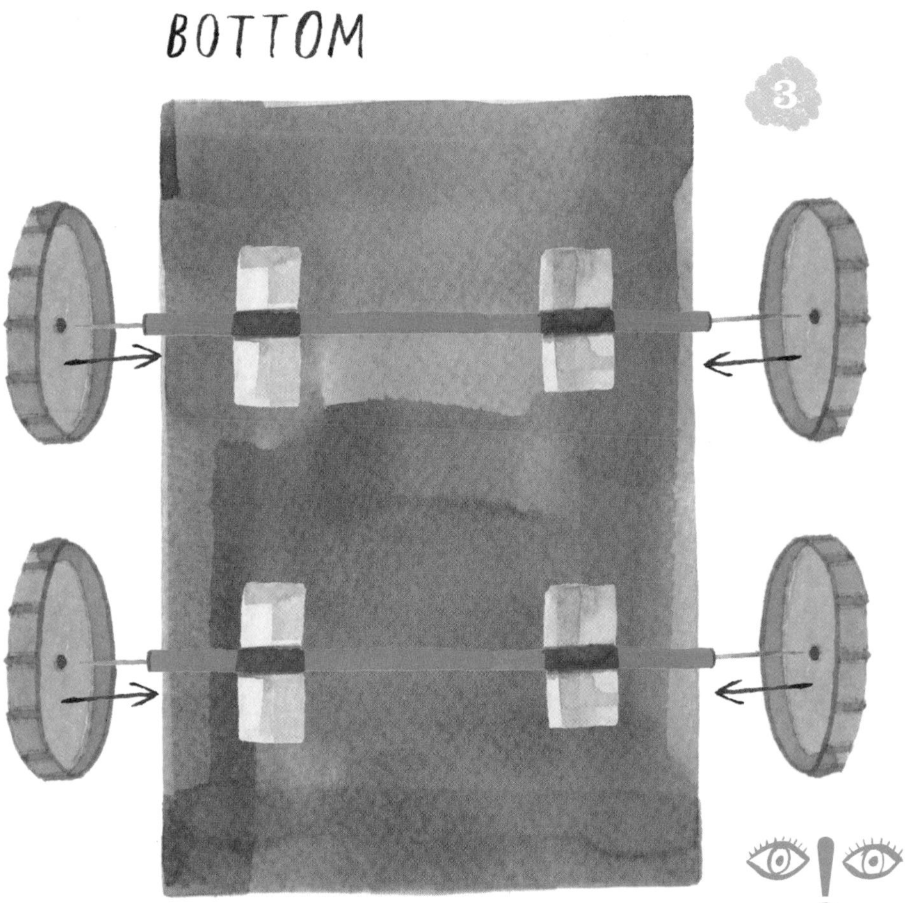
BOTTOM
3

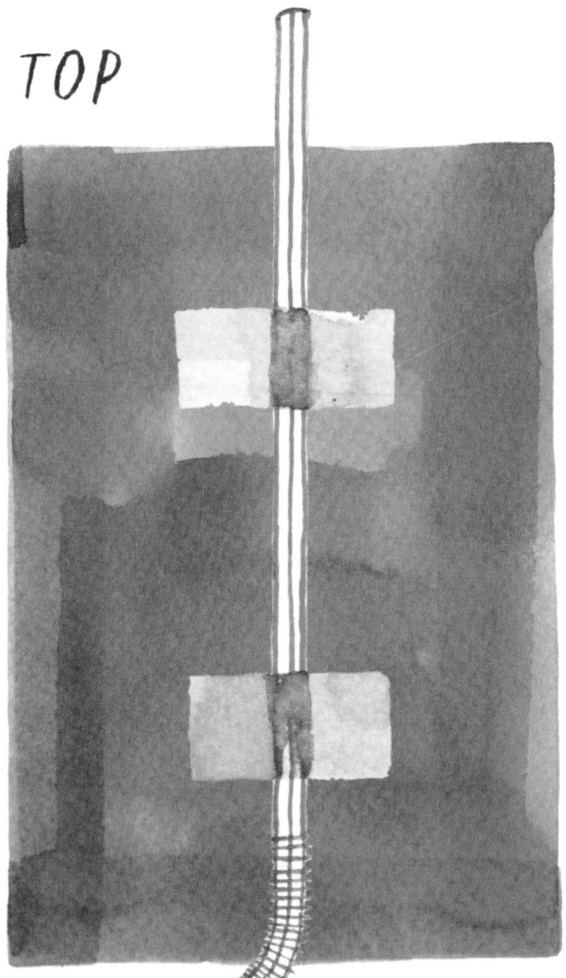
TOP

BE SAFE

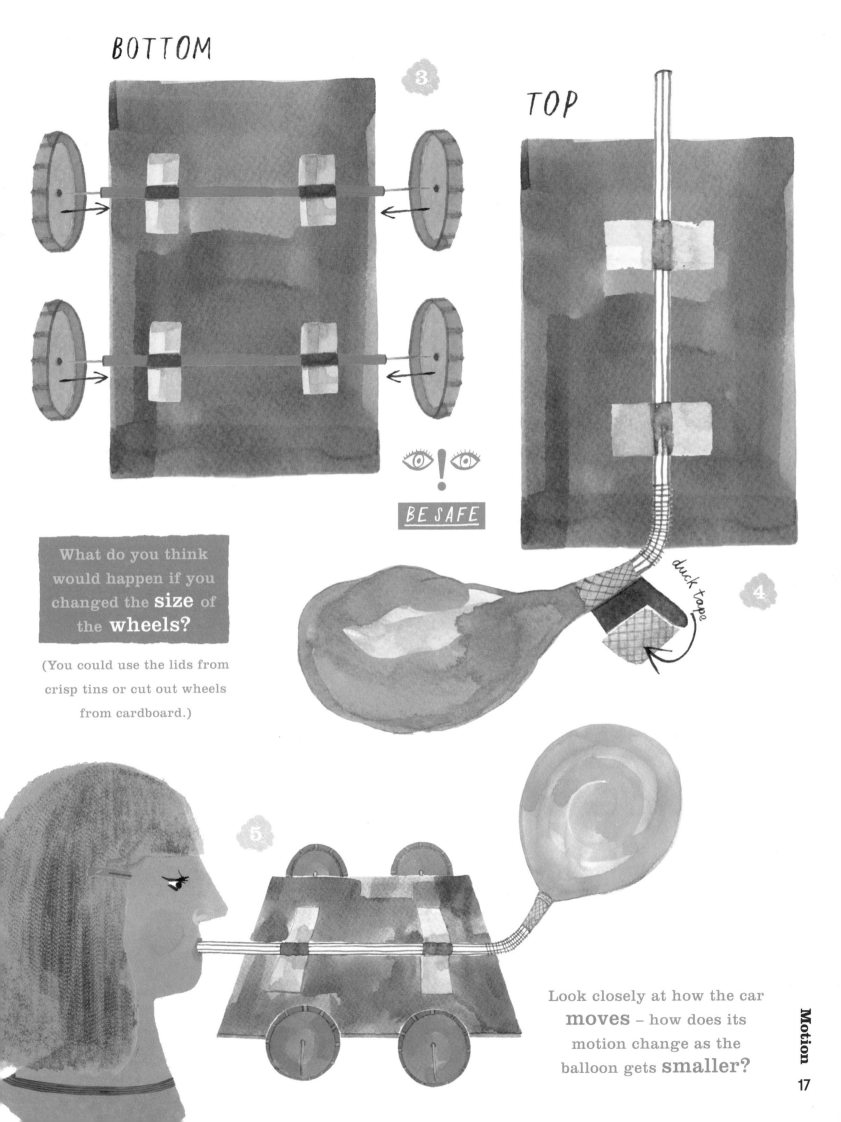

What do you think would happen if you changed the **size** of the **wheels?**

(You could use the lids from crisp tins or cut out wheels from cardboard.)

duck tape
4

5

Look closely at how the car **moves** – how does its motion change as the balloon gets **smaller?**

What could you change to make the car go further?
GO
ZOOM
What could you change to make the car go faster?
FINISH

In science, the **speed** of something is often measured in **metres per second.** To find the speed of your car, you would **divide** the **distance it travelled** in metres by the **time it took** to travel in seconds. Can **you** measure the speed of your car?

MR SHAHA says...

The balloon-powered cars illustrate two key ideas in science. The first is **Newton's First Law**, which states that **the motion of an object does not change** (whether it's at rest or moving) **unless the forces acting on it become unbalanced**.

Before the air is released from the balloon, all the forces acting on the car are balanced. When you take your finger off the end of the straw, the forces on the car become unbalanced and so it starts to move.

The second idea that the cars demonstrate is **Newton's Third Law**, which says that **forces always occur in pairs of equal size but acting in opposite directions**. So, if you push something, it will always push back on you with the same amount of force – but it's important to remember that the effect of these forces is not always the same because the forces act on different objects.

Sir Isaac Newton

Lots of things work like this – you walk by pushing backwards on the ground (which is why it's hard to walk on a slippery surface), the hot gases coming out of the back of a jet plane push it forwards, and when a bird flaps its wings it presses down on the air, which makes the bird go up.

You can't propel yourself backwards by blowing out of your mouth, or fly by flapping your arms; the forces of friction and gravity are too big in these situations. But if you go swimming and do breaststroke, your arms push the water backwards and that's what makes you move forwards – and that's **Newton's Third Law** in action!

In the case of the balloon cars, the inflated balloon pushes air out through the straw, meaning that the air pushes back on the balloon in the opposite direction. Since the balloon is attached to the car, the car moves forwards as the air moves backwards.

PLASTIC-BAG PARACHUTE

In 1783, Louis-Sébastien Lenormand used his own design for a parachute to jump safely from tower of the Montpellier observatory in France. We're not sure if he was the first person to use a parachute successfully, but he was the one who coined the word 'parachute', which combines the Latin prefix 'para', loosely meaning 'protection against', and the French word for fall, 'chute'. The parachute in this activity won't protect a human from falling, but might save an egg from breaking.

plastic carrier bag or small bin bag
empty yoghurt pot or plastic cup
string or thread at least 1m long
sellotape
an egg (optional)
scrap piece of cloth (optional)

INGREDIENTS

METHOD

1 Cut a 30 x30 cm square from your bag.

2 Cut four pieces of string, each 30 cm long.

3 Stick one end of each string to each corner of the yoghurt pot. Then stick the other end to a corner of the square.

4 Decide on your cargo. You can put anything you like inside your container, but using an egg can introduce an element of danger!

5 Find a safe, high place and drop your parachute!

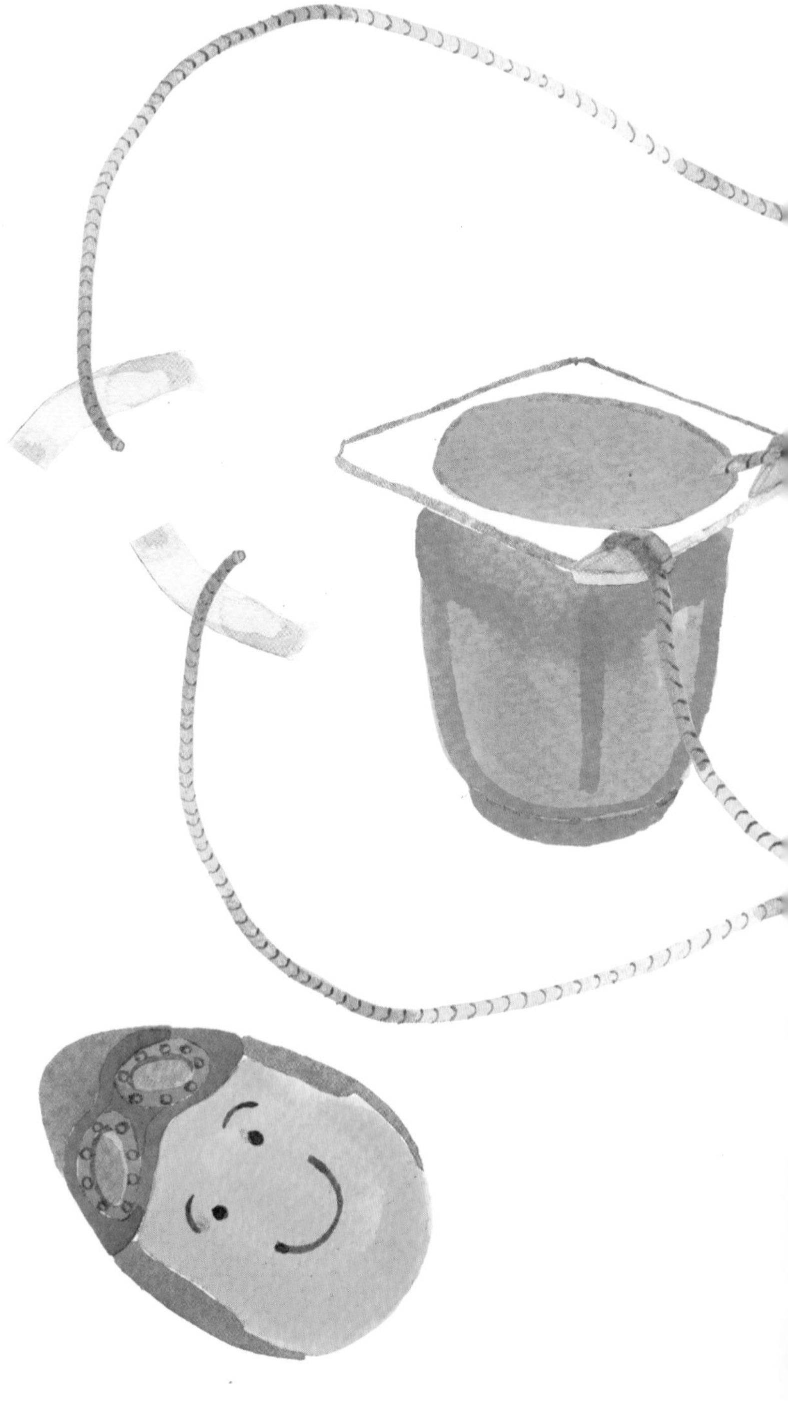

? What makes a **'good'** parachute? Is it how long it takes to hit the ground, or whether or not it protects the cargo?

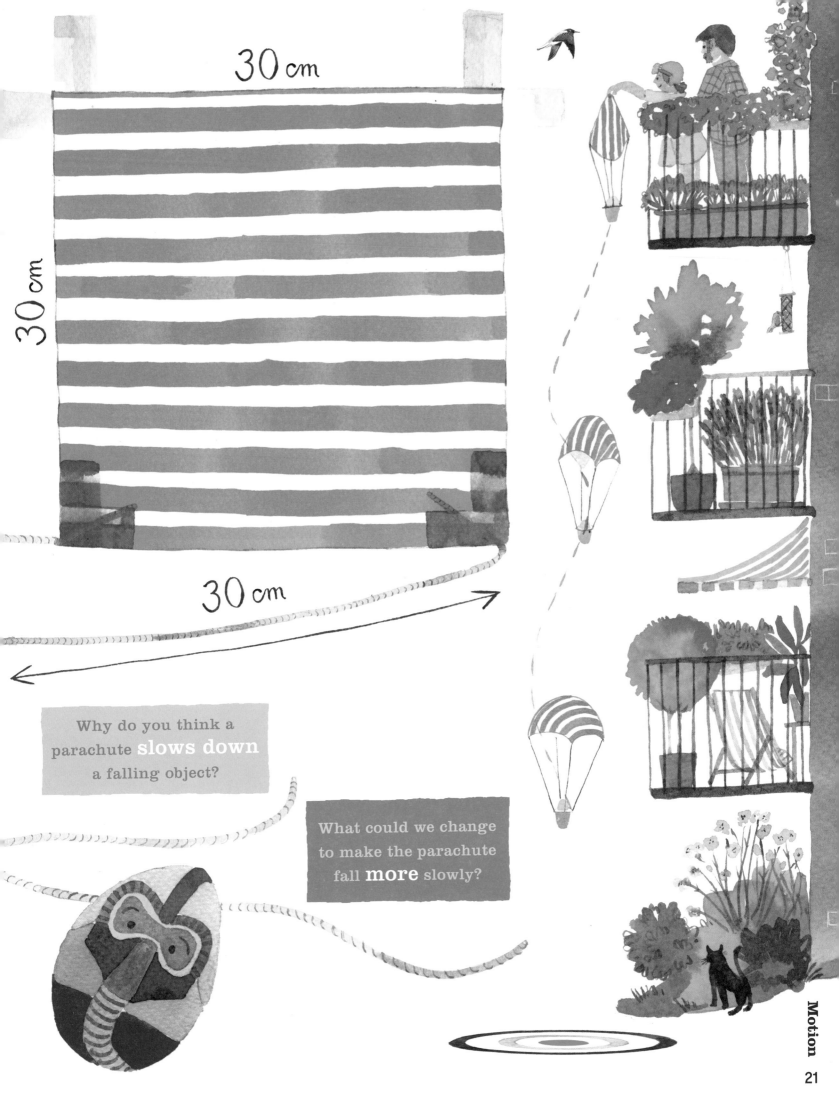

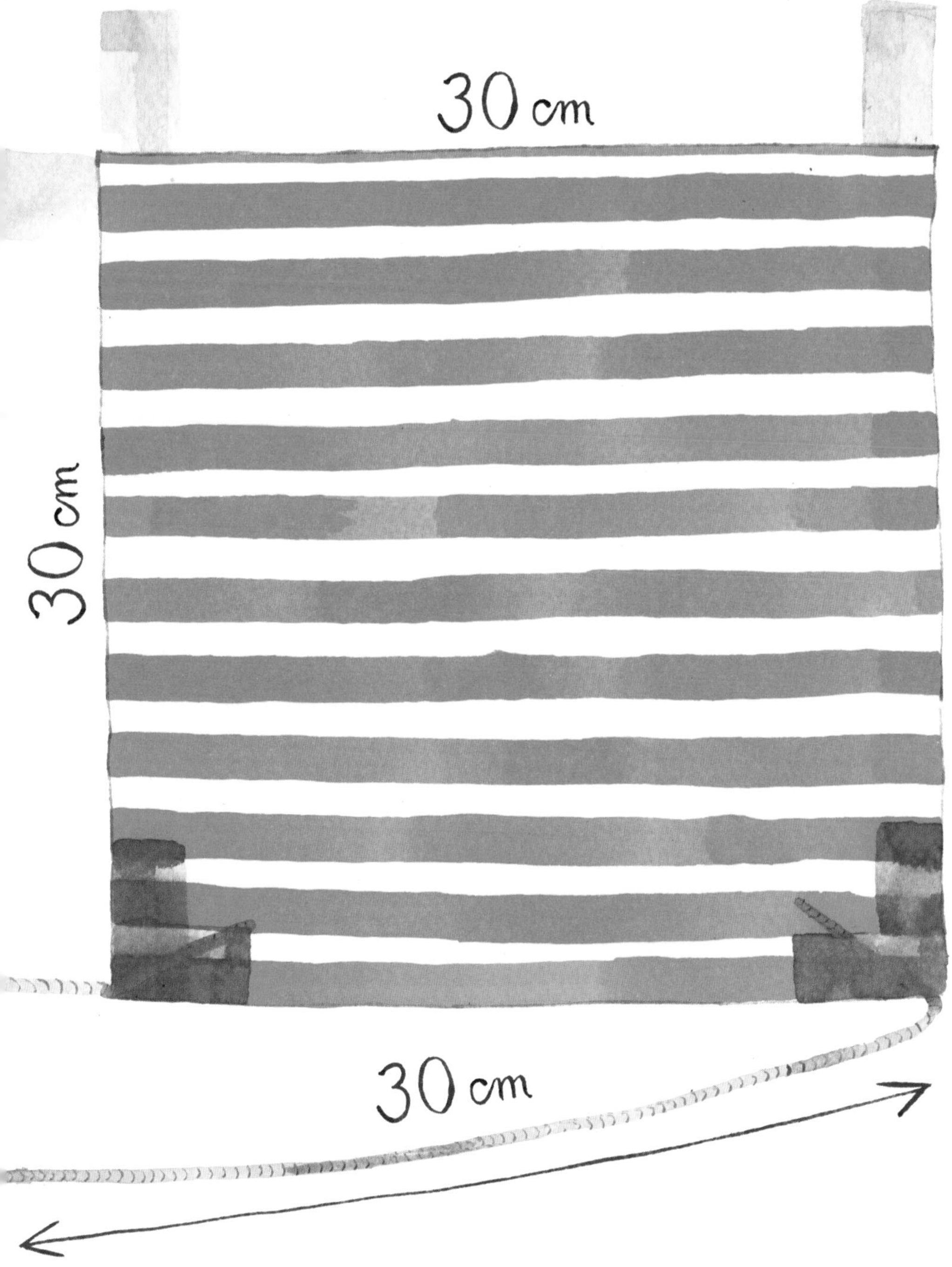
30 cm
30 cm
30 cm

Why do you think a parachute **slows down** a falling object?

What could we change to make the parachute fall **more** slowly?

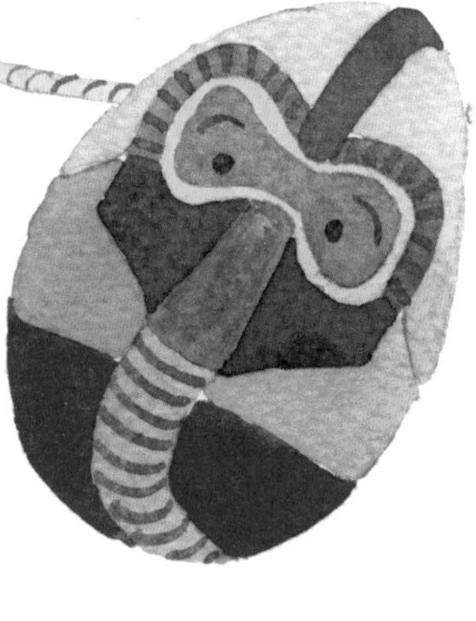

Do you think the **size** of a parachute makes a difference to how **quickly** it falls? Why? How could you find out?

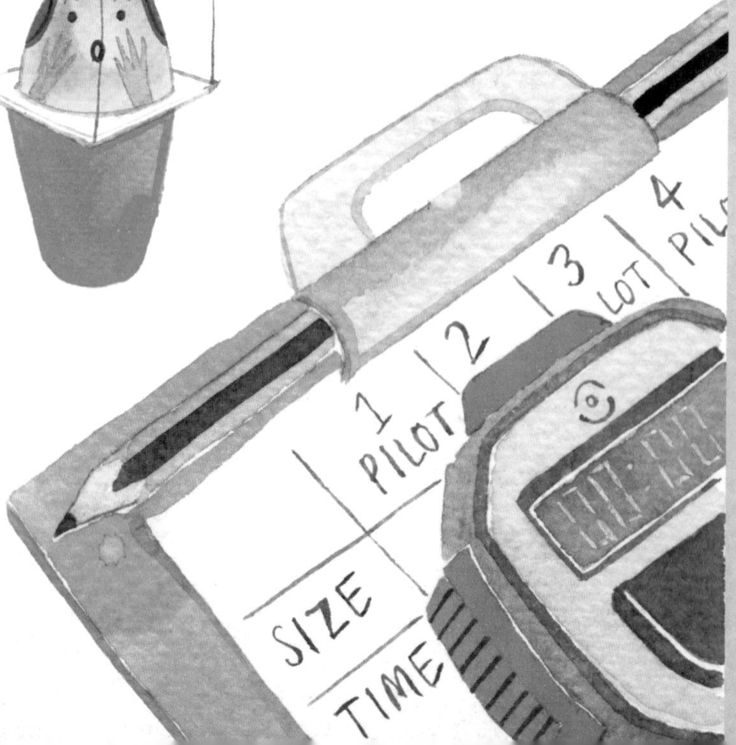
1 PILOT
2
3
4
SIZE
TIME

MR SHAHA says...

We don't usually notice the effect the air has on us when we're walking. But if it's really windy, or you stick a hand out of a moving car, you can feel that the air pushes against you in the opposite direction to which you're moving. This is called air resistance. A good parachute makes use of air resistance to slow down an object as it falls.

If you drop a crumpled ball of paper, it will fall more quickly through the air than a flat sheet.

That's because, even though they're the same weight, the flat paper has a bigger surface area and so has to push past more air. This slows it down. Things with a larger area experience more air resistance when they move through the air.

SOUND

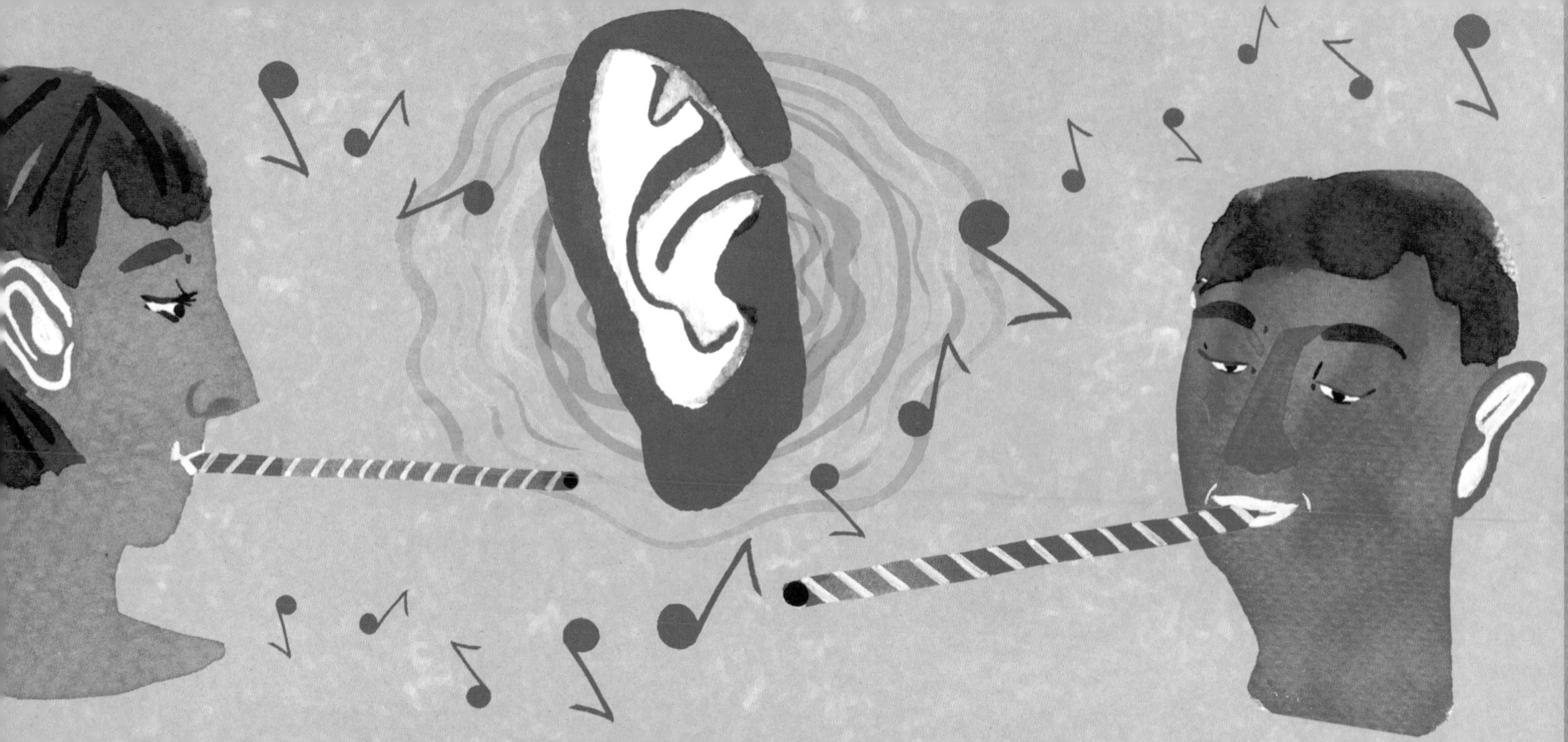

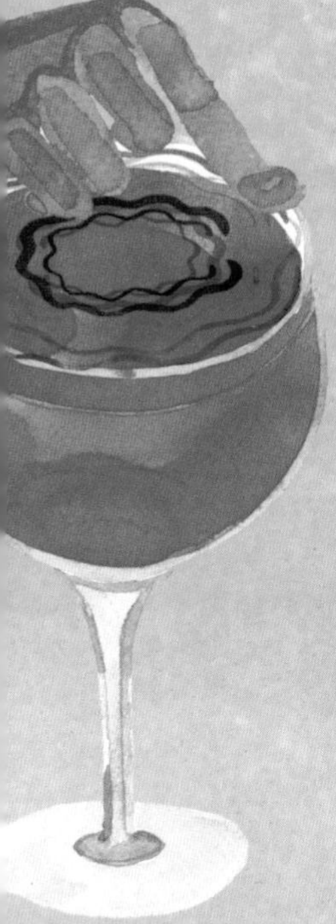

Sound is an incredibly useful natural phenomenon, central to how most of us experience the world and communicate. Sound is also what allows us to have music, which can engage us emotionally in a way that nothing else does.

When we scream or speak or sing, air from our lungs passes quickly over the vocal folds in our voice box, making them vibrate, which in turn makes the surrounding air vibrate. Those vibrations then travel through the air as waves, slowly dying away in size as they spread out.

For anyone to hear us, they need to be close enough for the vibrations in the air to reach their eardrums.

There are whole fields of science dedicated to the study of sound, and I've chosen the following activities to let you explore its properties and behaviour in fun and delightful ways.

MAGIC
TOYS

DRINKING-STRAW OBOE

One of my greatest regrets is that I never learnt to play a musical instrument as a child. I can't even whistle properly, but I'm pretty good at producing musical notes by blowing across the top of a bottle. There's something magical about being able to make music from household objects, and the straw oboe is a way of making an ordinary object produce an extraordinary sound.

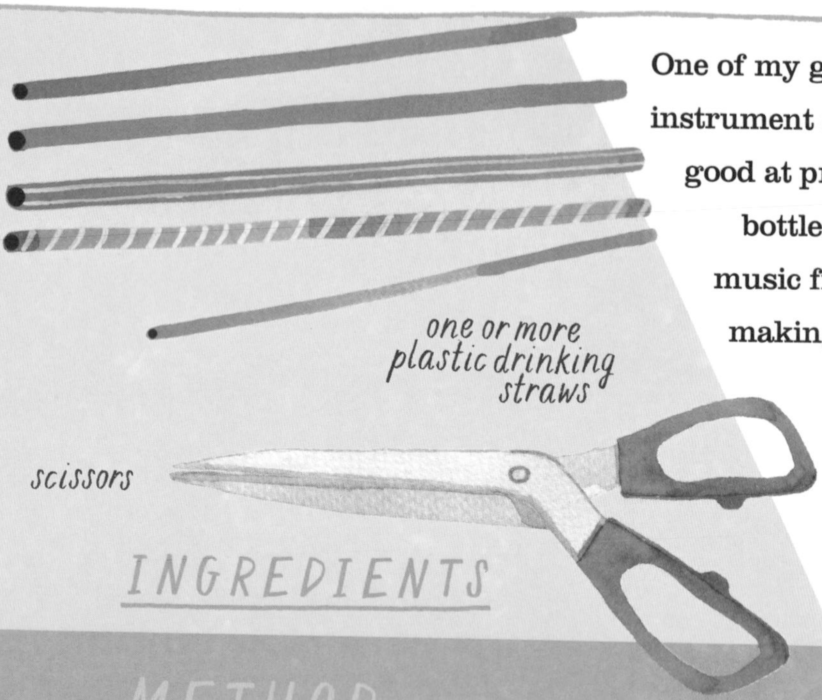
one or more plastic drinking straws
scissors

INGREDIENTS

METHOD

1 Bite down on one end of the straw, so that about 2 cm of it is in your mouth.

2 Pull the straw through your teeth so that you flatten the end. Repeat this a few times.

3 Cut the flattened end of the straw so that you have a triangle, as shown.

4 Place the pointy end of the straw in your mouth and blow – you should be able to produce a 'musical' note if you blow just hard enough. This may take some practice, but most people manage it within a few tries. If you can't make it work, try flattening the tip of the straw some more.

1

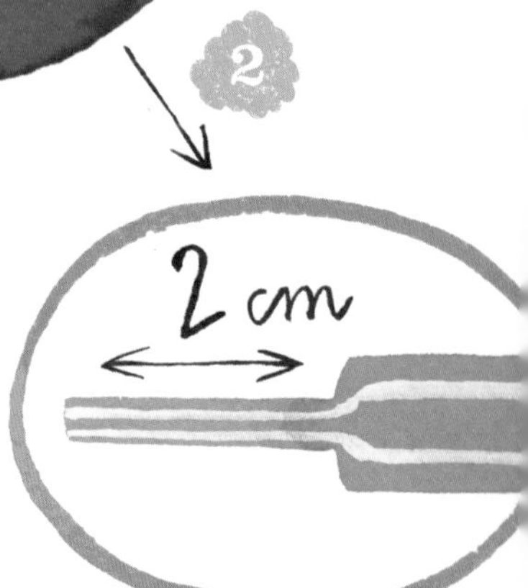
2
2 cm

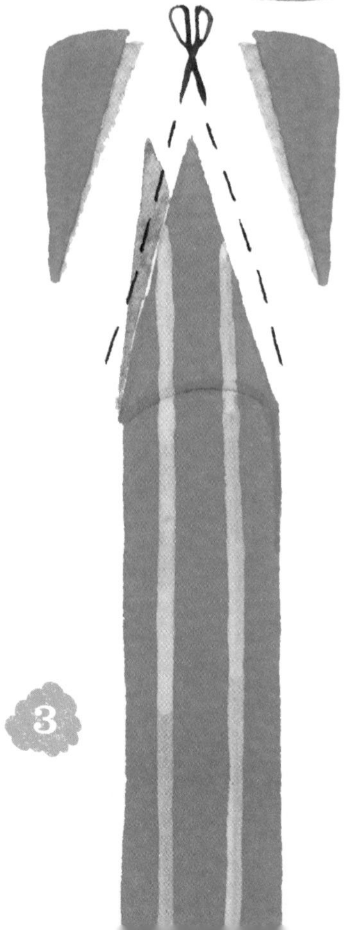
3

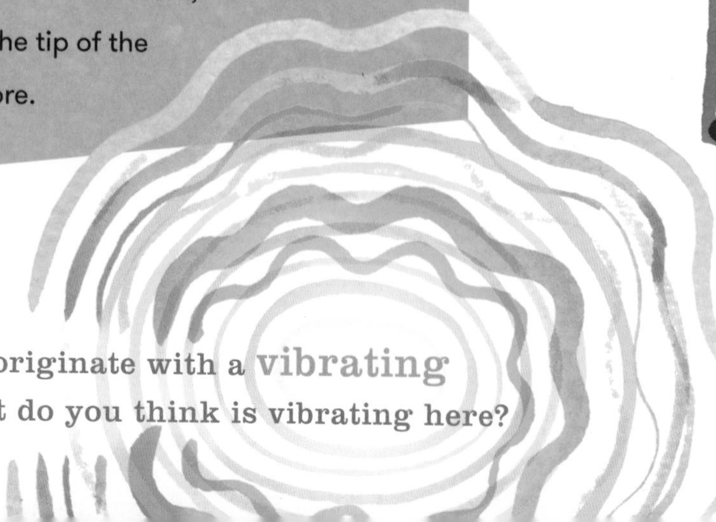

? All sounds originate with a **vibrating** object. What do you think is vibrating here?

What do you think would happen if you **cut** a short length off the bottom of your straw? Try it.

What happens if you use a **wider** or **narrower** straw?

Can you think of a way to use a **bunch** of straws together to make a musical instrument? (Hint: think of how pan pipes work).

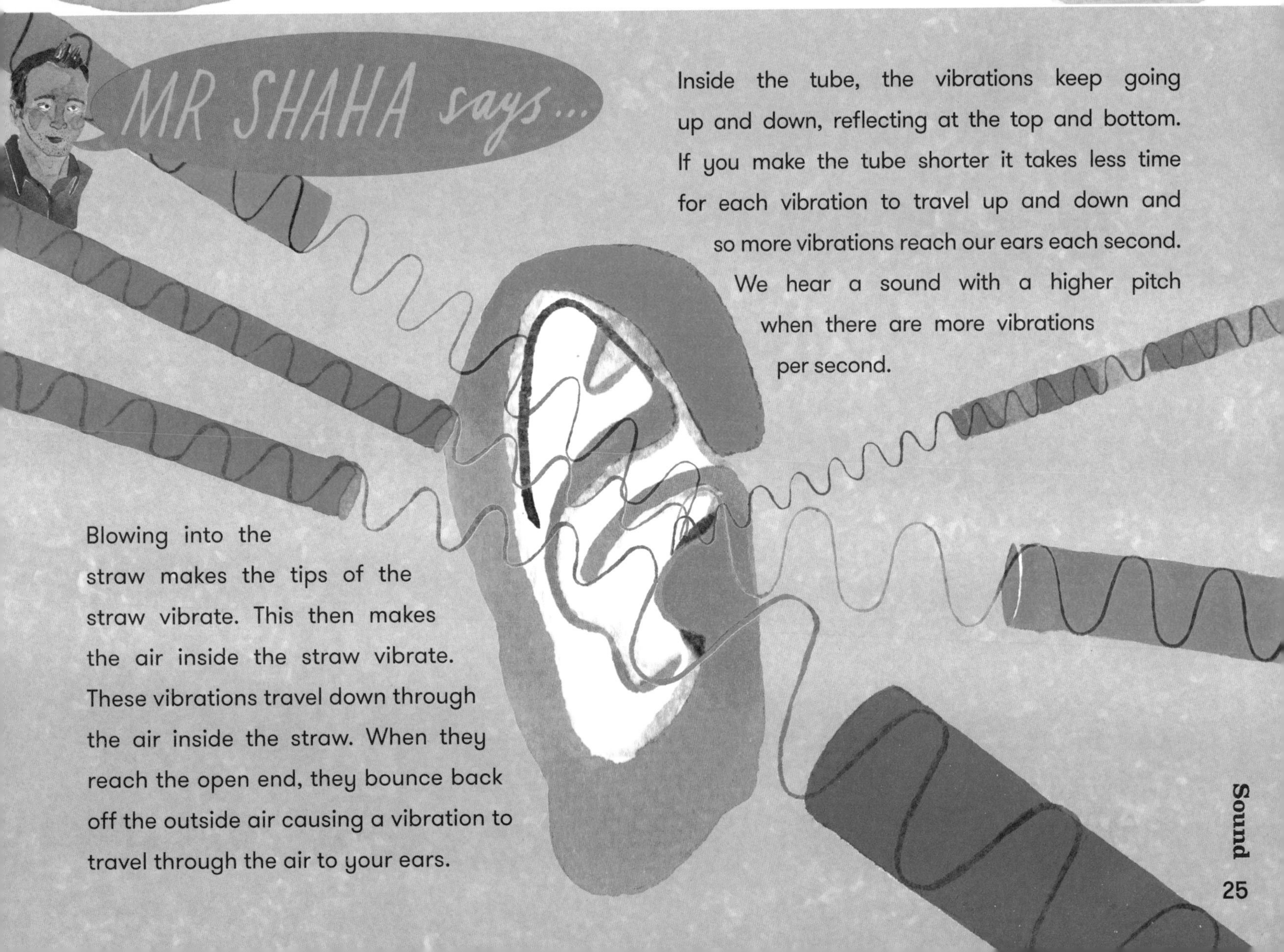

MR SHAHA says...

Inside the tube, the vibrations keep going up and down, reflecting at the top and bottom. If you make the tube shorter it takes less time for each vibration to travel up and down and so more vibrations reach our ears each second. We hear a sound with a higher pitch when there are more vibrations per second.

Blowing into the straw makes the tips of the straw vibrate. This then makes the air inside the straw vibrate. These vibrations travel down through the air inside the straw. When they reach the open end, they bounce back off the outside air causing a vibration to travel through the air to your ears.

HEAVY-METAL HANGERS

I love being introduced to new science demonstrations that I can use in my teaching. Despite being a physics teacher, and kind of knowing what to expect, I was astonished the first time I tried this – it is a truly startling demonstration of the way sounds are produced and how they travel.

metal coathanger (the thicker ones work best) or metal oven rack
2 pieces of string or wool 50–75 cm long

INGREDIENTS

METHOD

1 Tie a piece of string to each end of the base of your hanger or to the corners of your oven rack.

2 Holding it by the strings, bang the object against a table leg or chair and listen to the sound it makes.

? **Is the sound what you expected?**

3 Next, loop a few centimetres of each string around the ends of each of your index fingers.

4 Put one finger in each ear so that your metal object hangs down in front of you.

? **What do you expect to hear now if you hit the object against the table?**

5 Try it!

2

? **Why do you think what you hear is so different when you do it like this?**

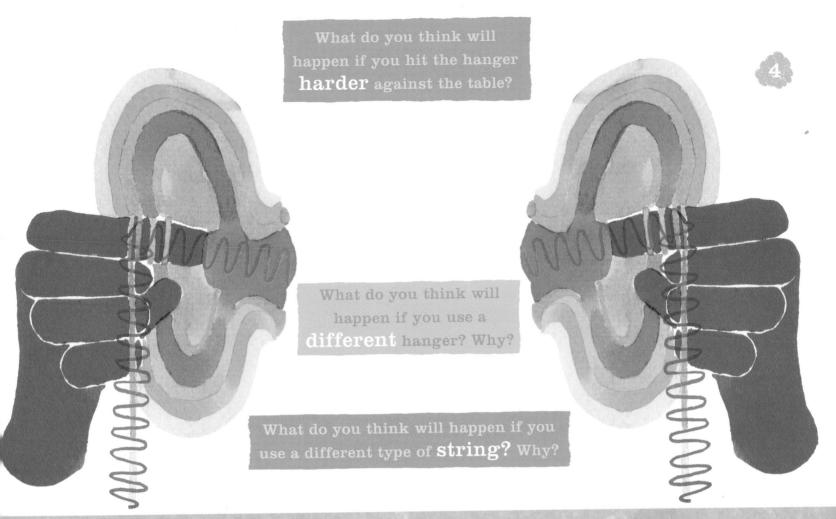

What do you think will happen if you hit the hanger **harder** against the table?

4

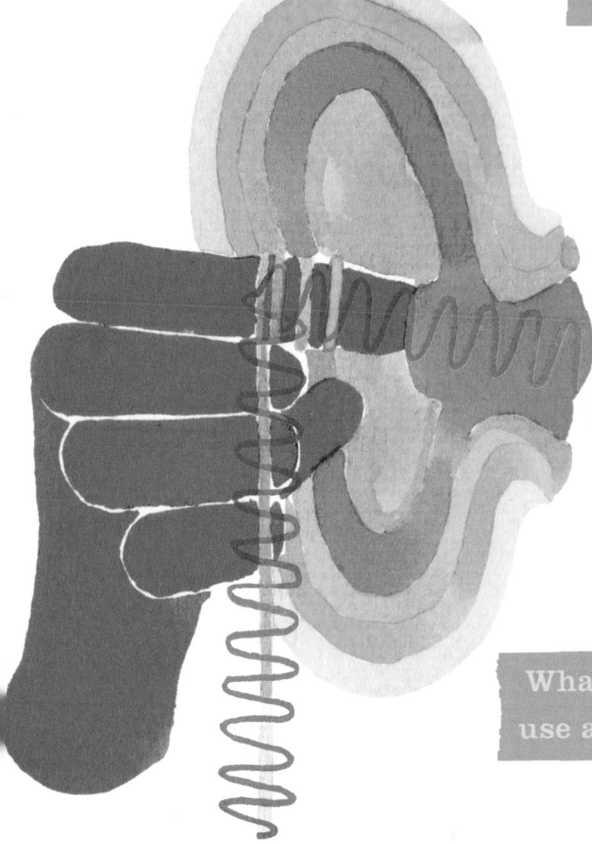

What do you think will happen if you use a **different** hanger? Why?

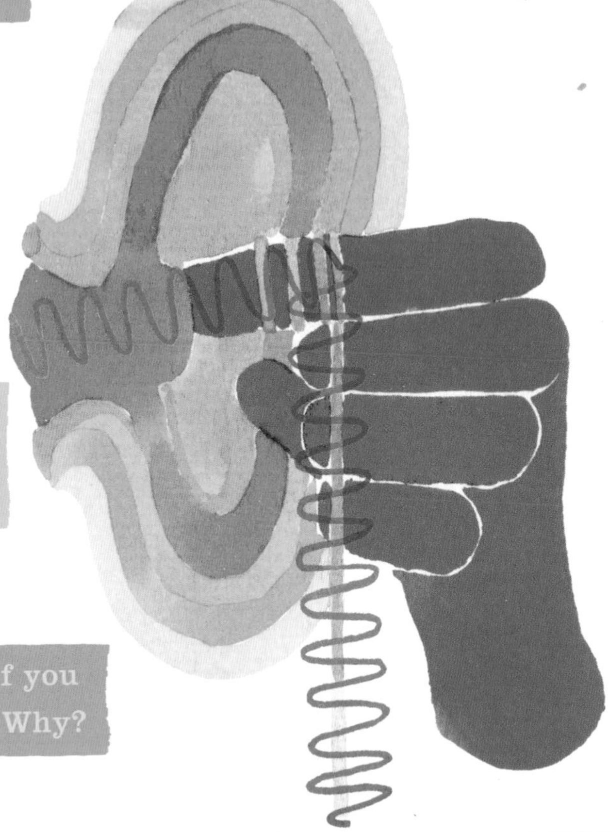

What do you think will happen if you use a different type of **string?** Why?

MR SHAHA says...

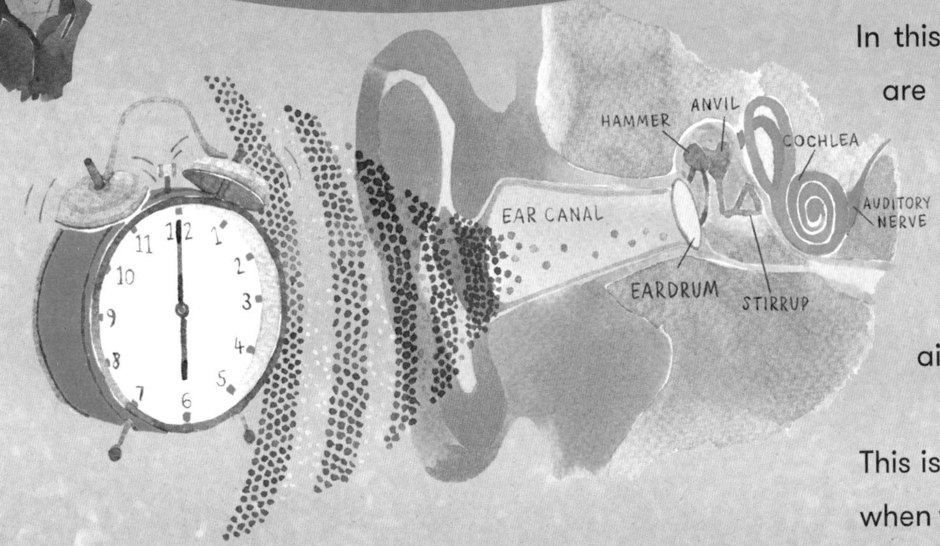
HAMMER
ANVIL
COCHLEA
EAR CANAL
AUDITORY NERVE
EARDRUM
STIRRUP

Sounds are made when objects vibrate. It's not always obvious, but if something is making a sound, some part of it must be vibrating.

The precise way in which the object vibrates determines the sound we hear. Usually, we hear sounds because the vibration of the object makes the air around it vibrate, and those vibrations travel through the air and make our ear drums vibrate.

In this case, the vibrations of the coat hanger are passed onto the string, and then onto your finger. Since your finger is inside your ear, vibrations are passed onto your ear drum through the flesh and bone of your head as well as through the air inside the ear canal.

This is why our own voices sound different to us when we hear a recording – we are hearing them through the air when we are used to hearing them through our solid skulls.

MAGIC
TOYS

SINGING WINE GLASSES

For one of my school science projects, I investigated what happened to the size of a splatter made by a drop of ink when it fell from different heights. My friend Angharad did a much more interesting and sophisticated experiment, which is where I first came across the phenomenon at the heart of this activity. What makes something music instead of just a sound? I'm not sure whether that's a philosophical or scientific question, or both, but this activity might help you come to your own conclusions.

towel or tissues
jug of water
one or more wine glasses
plastic pen or pencil
one or more glass tumblers

INGREDIENTS

METHOD

1 Before you begin the activity, use your pen or pencil to gently tap the glasses one at a time and see what sounds they make. Pick a wine glass you like the sound of for the next part of the activity.

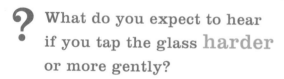

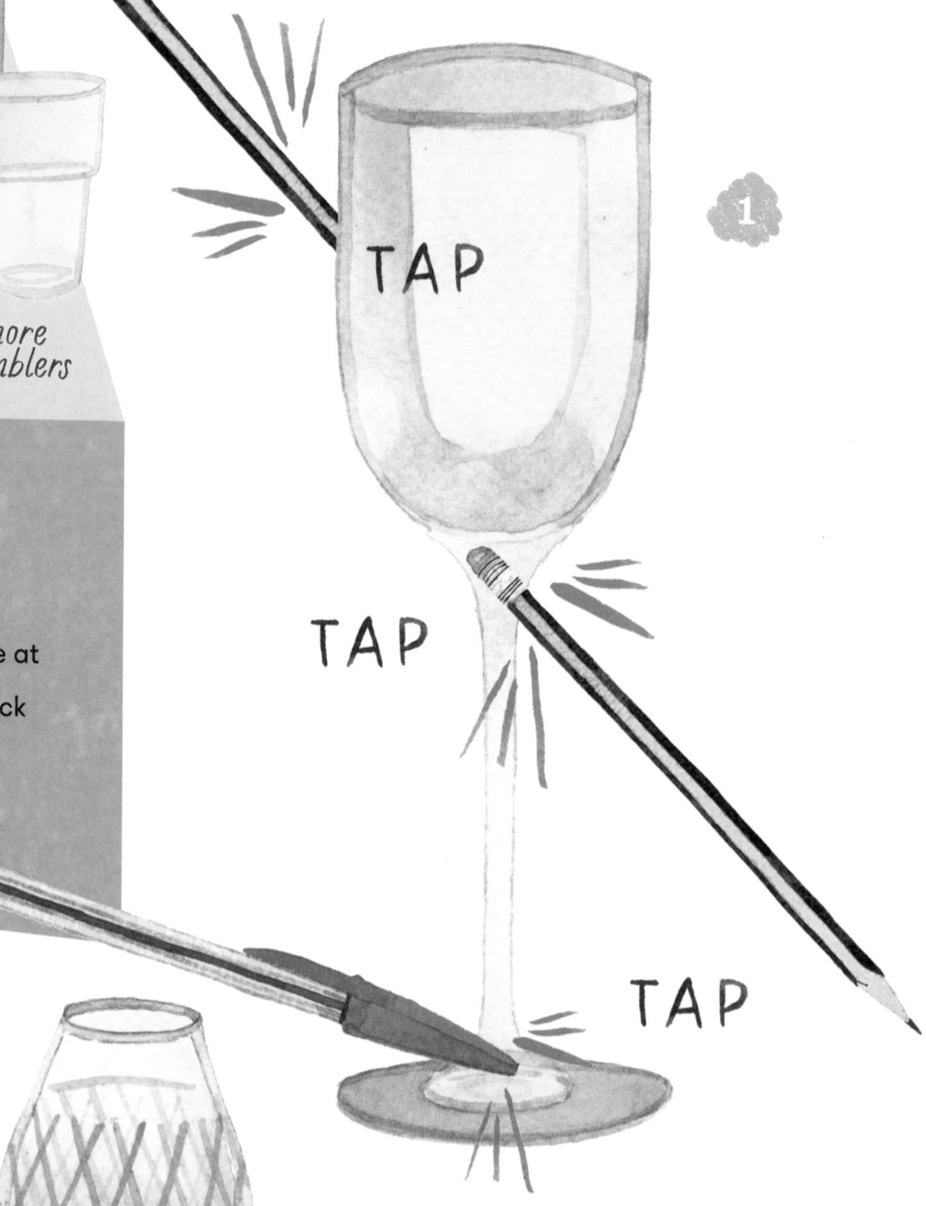

1
TAP
TAP
TAP

? What do you expect to hear if you tap the glass harder or more gently?

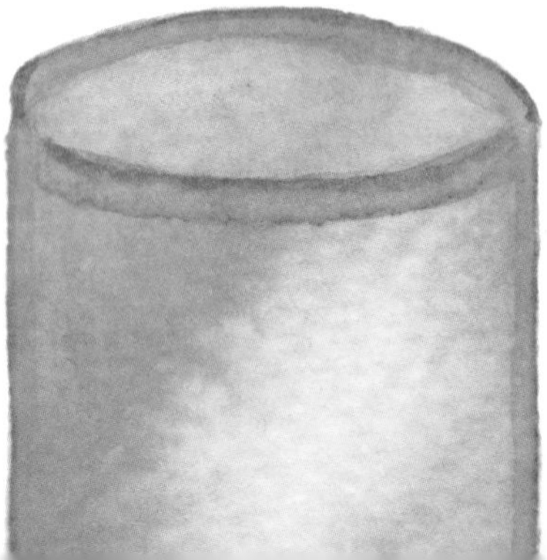

What do you expect to hear if you tap the stem or base of the glass?

What do you expect to hear if you pour a little **water** in the glass before tapping it?

(Make sure you tap the glass as hard or as gently as you did last time, to ensure that you're doing a 'fair test')

What do you expect to hear if you pour **more** water in the glass before tapping it?

2 Hold your chosen wine glass (empty) firmly down on the table with one hand. Dip the tip of the index finger of your other hand in some water and press it down firmly, but not too hard, on the rim of the glass.

3 Still pressing down, run your finger slowly around the rim so that you complete about one revolution (a full circle around the rim of the glass) a second. You should be able to make the wine glass produce a musical note in this way.

3

? What do you think will happen if you **press** a little harder?

What do you think will happen if you run your fingers around more **quickly**?

What do you think will happen if you try this with **water** added to the glass? How does this change the sound?

Can you add **just enough** water to a glass to make a particular note?

Could you use **more than one** glass and play a tune?

MR SHAHA says...

When we hit a glass, it makes a sound because it vibrates. All sounds are made by making something vibrate. Different objects vibrate in different ways depending on how they are being made to move, and the sound you hear depends on exactly how the object is vibrating. Changing the amount of water in the glass changes the way it vibrates and this changes the note you hear.

When you run a wet finger around the rim of a glass, it repeatedly sticks and then slides. This makes the glass vibrate and produce a sound. When you do this with water in the glass, both the water and the glass vibrate. Try it with a really full glass – look closely to see ripples on the surface of the water!

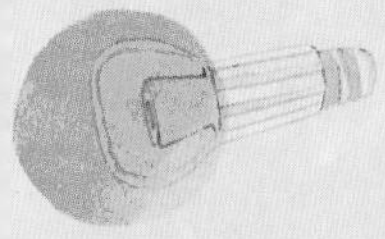

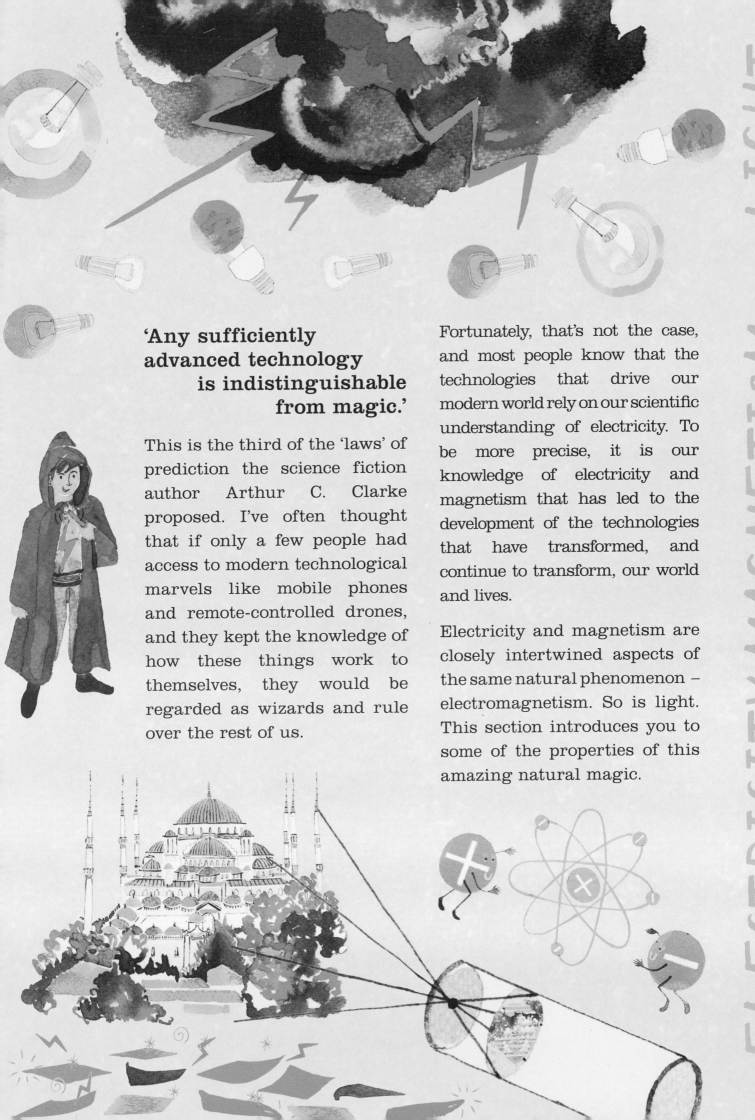

'Any sufficiently advanced technology is indistinguishable from magic.'

This is the third of the 'laws' of prediction the science fiction author Arthur C. Clarke proposed. I've often thought that if only a few people had access to modern technological marvels like mobile phones and remote-controlled drones, and they kept the knowledge of how these things work to themselves, they would be regarded as wizards and rule over the rest of us.

Fortunately, that's not the case, and most people know that the technologies that drive our modern world rely on our scientific understanding of electricity. To be more precise, it is our knowledge of electricity and magnetism that has led to the development of the technologies that have transformed, and continue to transform, our world and lives.

Electricity and magnetism are closely intertwined aspects of the same natural phenomenon – electromagnetism. So is light. This section introduces you to some of the properties of this amazing natural magic.

SIMPLE ELECTRIC MOTOR

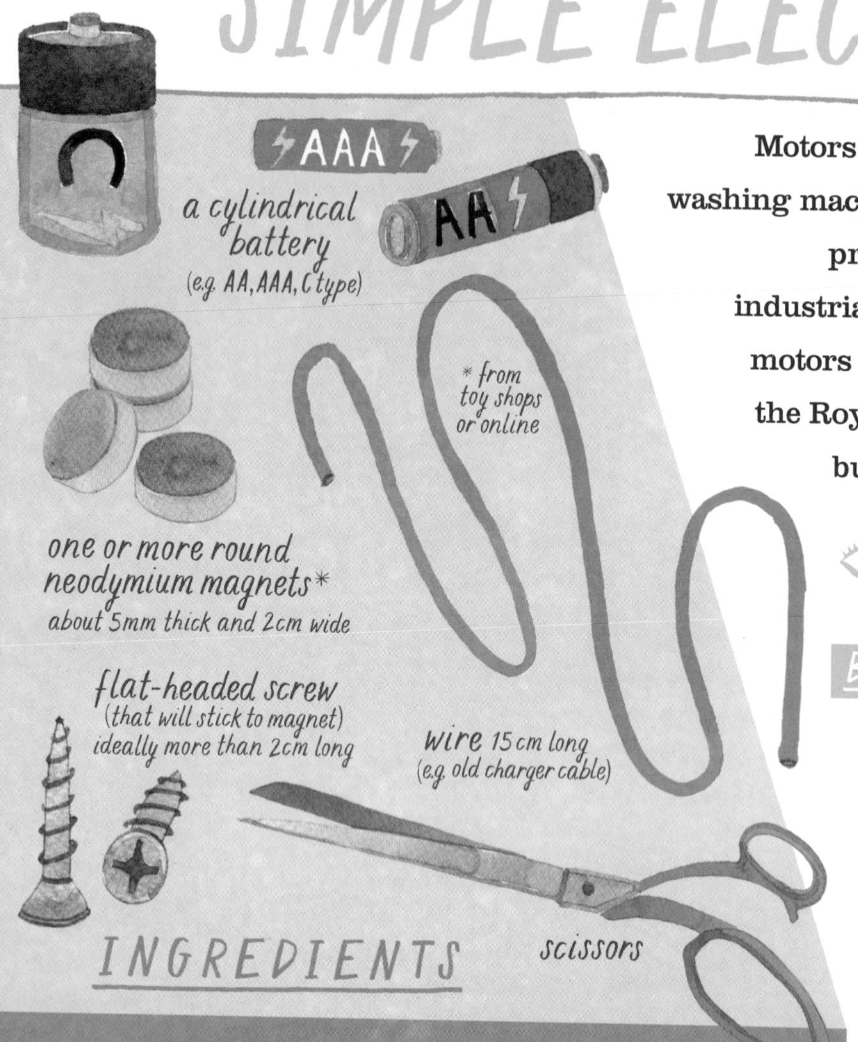
AAA
AA
a cylindrical battery
(e.g. AA, AAA, C type)
one or more round neodymium magnets*
about 5mm thick and 2cm wide
* from toy shops or online
flat-headed screw
(that will stick to magnet)
ideally more than 2cm long
wire 15 cm long
(e.g. old charger cable)
scissors

INGREDIENTS

Motors make our lives easier. They are at the heart of every washing machine, dishwasher, lawnmower, vacuum cleaner, food processor, and countless other household gadgets and industrial machinery. The basic principle that makes electric motors work was discovered in 1821 by Michael Faraday at the Royal Institution in London. This activity allows you to build your own simple, but impressive, electric motor.

BE SAFE

A QUICK NOTE ABOUT SAFETY:
Do not keep the wire in contact with the battery for too long, as it may become unpleasantly hot or cause the insulation on it to melt.

METHOD

1 If you're using insulated wire, strip 1 cm or so of the insulation off from each end by gently cutting round the plastic with scissors.

2 Stick the head of the screw to one of the flat sides of the magnet.

3 Hold the battery and put the point of the screw to the bottom end – it should stay in place due to the magnetism from the magnet.

4 Use a finger from the same hand you're holding the battery in to hold one end of the wire against the top of the battery.

5 Using your other hand, bring the other end of the wire into contact with the side of the magnet.

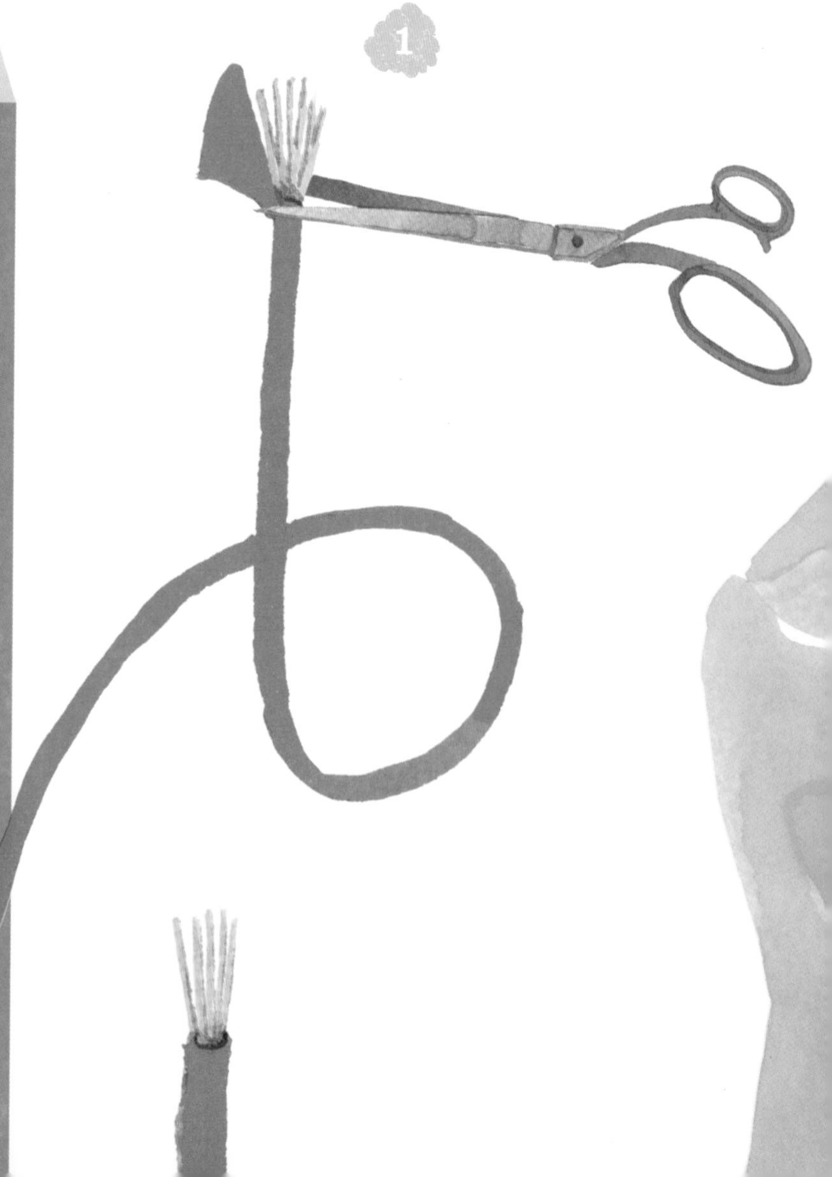
1

What do you think will happen if you add **another** magnet to the bottom of the first one?

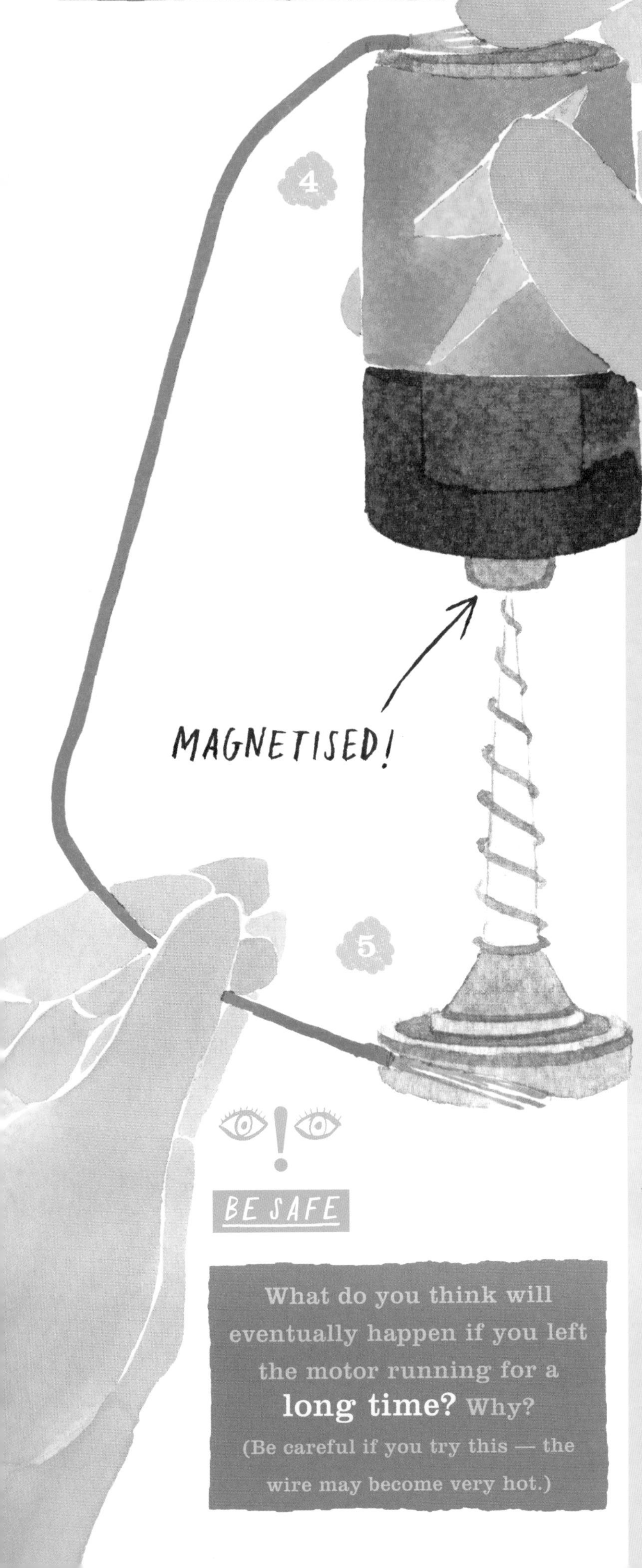
4
MAGNETISED!
5

BE SAFE

What do you think will eventually happen if you left the motor running for a **long time?** Why?

(Be careful if you try this — the wire may become very hot.)

MR SHAHA says...

Magnets push or pull other magnets and certain metals like iron, cobalt and nickel. When you pass electricity through something, it becomes magnetic and so will experience a force if it is placed near a magnet. In this activity, the magnet and screw are made of metal, which allows electricity to flow through them.

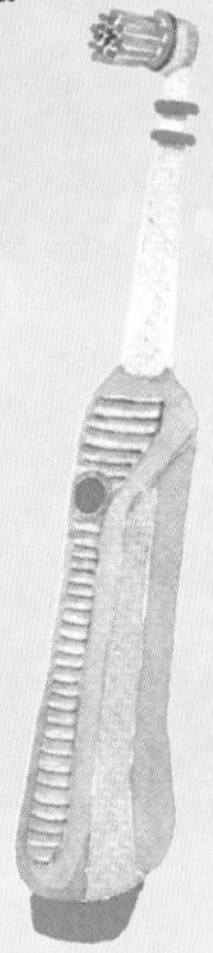

Touching the wire to the side of the magnet completes an electric circuit so that a current can flow.

Now there are two magnetic fields: the one produced by the current and the other produced by the magnet. These fields push against each other just as can happen when you bring two magnets close together. This push makes the magnet spin.

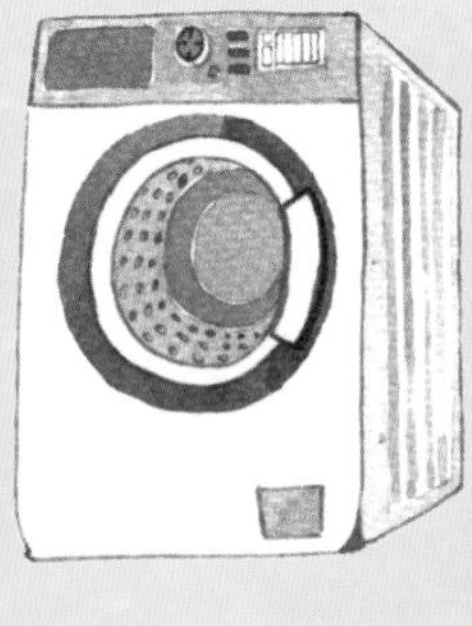

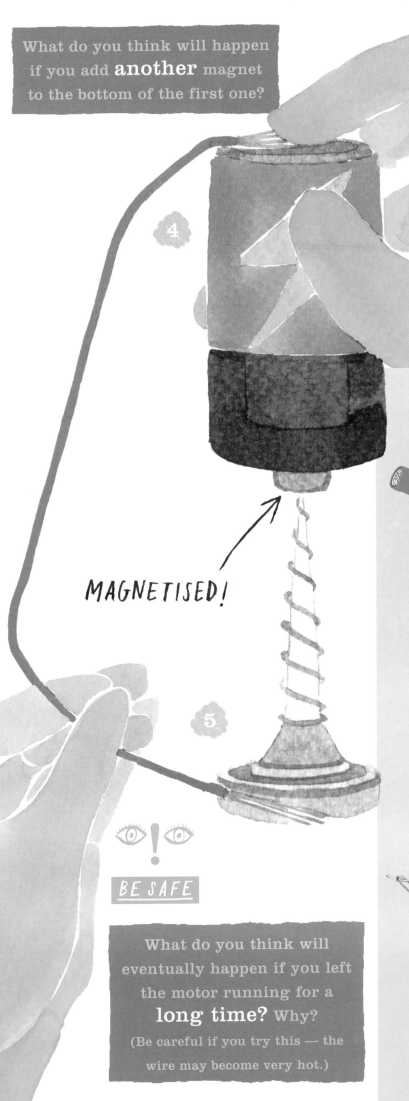

CRISP-TIN CAMERA

The first cameras did not take photographs, instead they were darkened rooms (a 'camera obscura' in Latin), where images of the outside world were projected onto a wall. This activity lets you build your own camera obscura and introduces some important ideas about the behaviour of light.

CRISPS
scissors
masking tape
or sellotape
magnifying lens
or pair of glasses
(optional)
drawing pin/safety pin
cardboard
crisp tube
with lid
marker
pen
ruler
TINFOIL
greaseproof or
tracing paper
10x10 cm
GREASE PROOF
foil
at least 25 cm long
a sunny day

INGREDIENTS

METHOD

1 Remove the lid and wipe out the tin. Draw a line around it, 5 cm from the unopened end. Carefully cut along it, leaving two tubes.

2 Use the pin to make a hole in the middle of the bottom of the shorter tube.

3 Place the paper over the open end of the shorter tube and put the lid on firmly.

4 Fold down the edges of the paper and tape all the way round so that it is stuck to the tube (avoid sticking the lid). Remove the lid.

5 Using tape, fix the two tubes back together so that the paper screen is inside the tube. (Go round twice with the tape to make it secure).

6 Wrap foil around the side of the tube and use tape to secure it. Run some tape around each end to fix the foil so no light gets in.

7 Point the pinhole out of a window and look through the other end of the tube (cup your hands around the tube to keep out light). You may need to wait for your eyes to become accustomed to the dark.

8 Try using your phone to take photographs through the camera obscura.

1

? Why do you think you need a **bright sunny day** to do this activity?

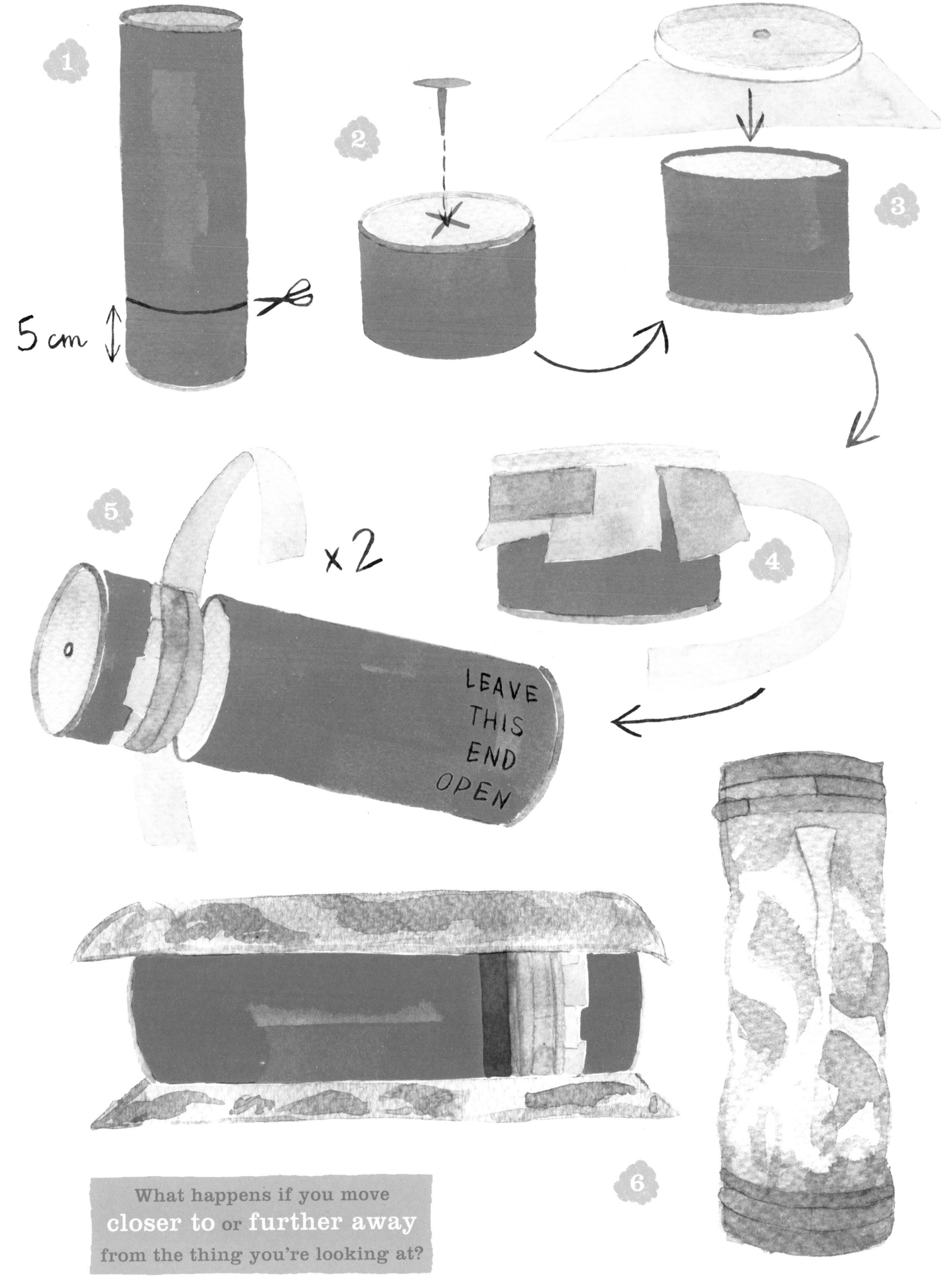
1
5 cm
2
3
4
5
x2
LEAVE THIS END OPEN
6

What happens if you move **closer to** or **further away** from the thing you're looking at?

What do you notice about the image you see in the camera?
What do you think would happen if you make the hole bigger?
What happens if you put a magnifying lens in front of the hole?

MR SHAHA says...

The image we see on the screen is upside down because of the way light travels into the tin through the small pinhole. Emily's picture below helps us to understand what's going on.

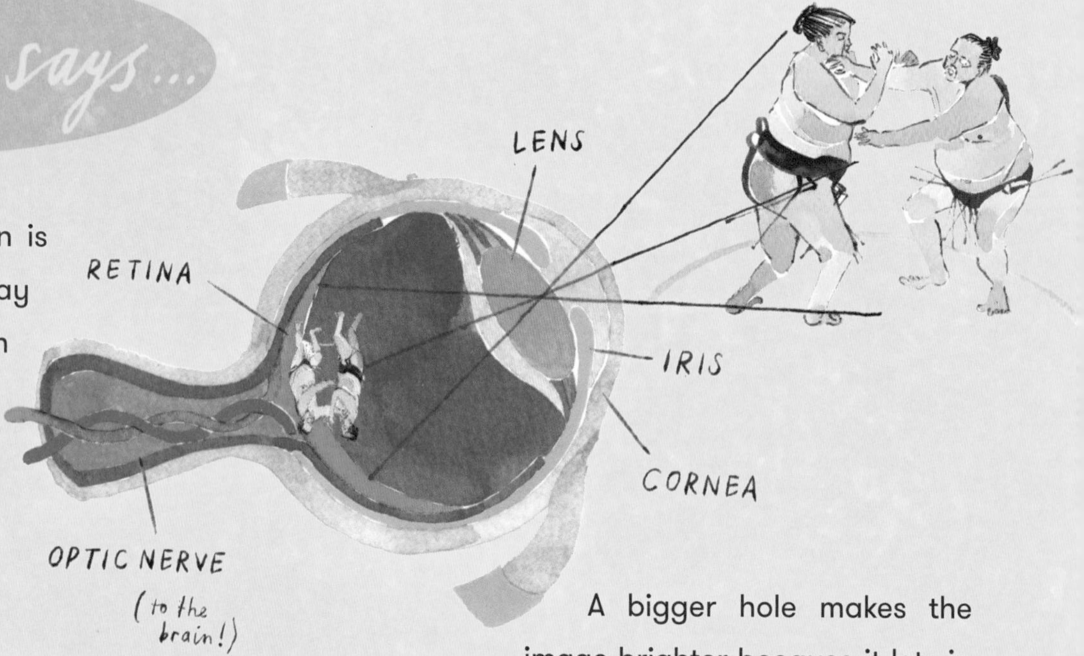
LENS
RETINA
IRIS
CORNEA
OPTIC NERVE
(to the brain!)

Light travels in straight lines. Because the object is so much bigger than the pinhole, light from the top of the object moves downwards as it goes through the pinhole, so it ends up on the bottom of the screen, whereas light from the bottom of the object moves upwards through the pinhole and ends up on the top of the screen.

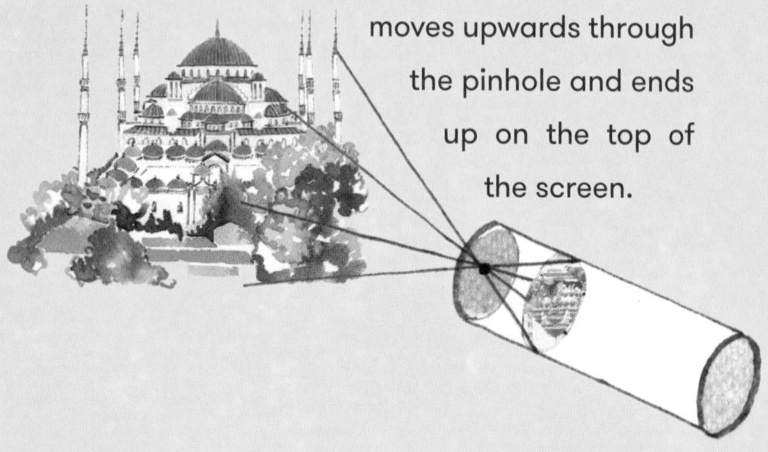

A bigger hole makes the image brighter because it lets in more rays of light, but also blurrier because more rays overlap. Most objects don't produce their own light and we only see them when they reflect light from ones that do. This is why you need a bright day to get decent images.

Eyeballs are like a camera obscura, with a hole at the front (the pupil) and a screen at the back (the retina). The image formed at the back of our eyes is upside down, but our brains flip it so we see things the right way up.

RAINBOW TUBE

scissors
cardboard crisp tube with lid
CRISPS
foil
TINFOIL
bread knife
(or any with serrated edge)
CD or DVD
(that looks silver, not blue)
glue stick

INGREDIENTS

Looking closely at things helps us learn more about the world, but sometimes our eyes alone are not enough. Scientists have invented various instruments to help us see things that would otherwise not be visible, like telescopes that allow us to look at objects that are huge distances away, and microscopes which allow us to see incredibly tiny things. In this activity, you'll make a spectroscope, an instrument that allows us to analyse light by splitting it up into colours.

BE SAFE

A QUICK NOTE ABOUT SAFETY:
Never point your spectroscope directly at the sun, instead, point it at a bright bit of the sky.

METHOD

1 Remove the lid from a clean tube and set aside.

2 Starting 6 cm from the closed end of the tube, cut a slot for the CD. The slot should be at a 45-degree angle to the side of the tube and to a depth of about half the width of the tube, as shown.

3 Use the scissors to make a peephole in the tube directly across from the middle of the slit.

turn the page »

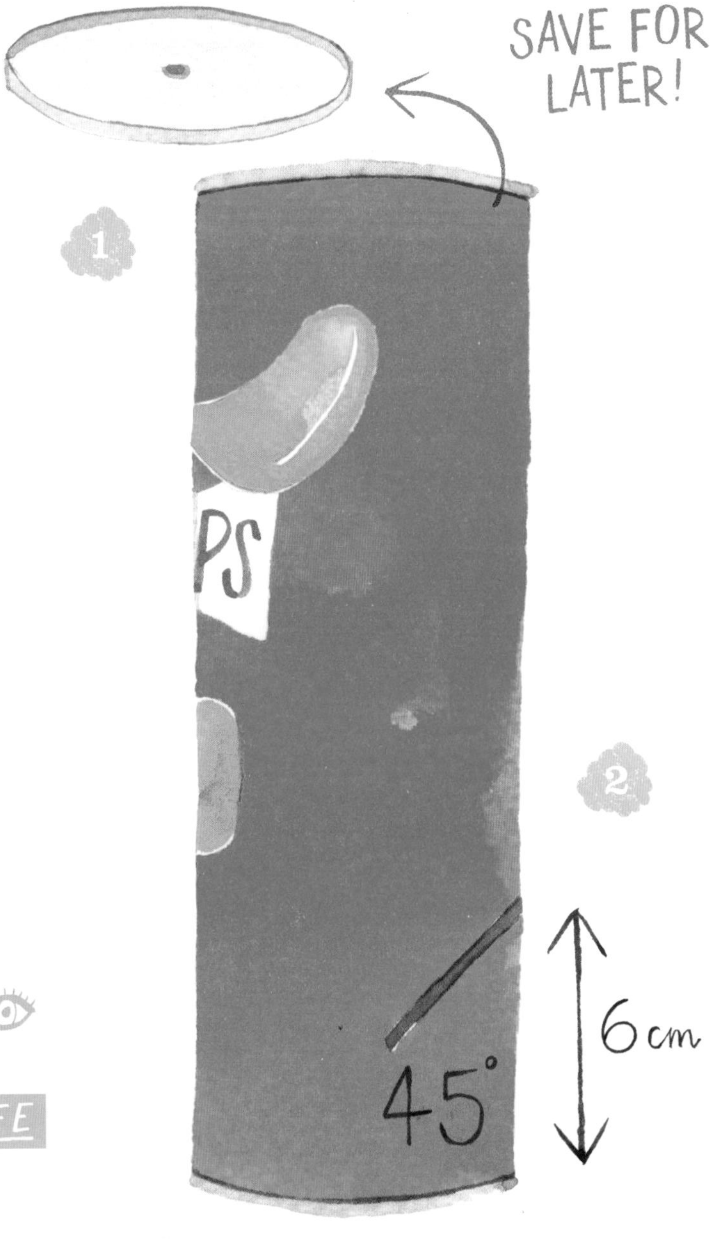

SAVE FOR LATER!
1
PS
2
45°
6 cm

3
CRISP

BE SAFE

4 Put the CD into the slot so that the silver side points upwards, towards the open end of the tube.

5 Cut a 20 cm wide sheet of foil and wrap it around the CD so that the slot is completely covered up.

6 Glue a sheet of foil to the inside of the lid so that it is completely covered. Cut a thin slit into the lid, 2 mm wide and 6 cm long.

7 Place the lid on the tube so the slit is horizontal when the tube is placed on its side and the peep hole is facing upwards.

8 Your spectroscope is ready for use – point the slit at a source of light, like the sky, a light bulb, or a candle flame, and look through the peephole.

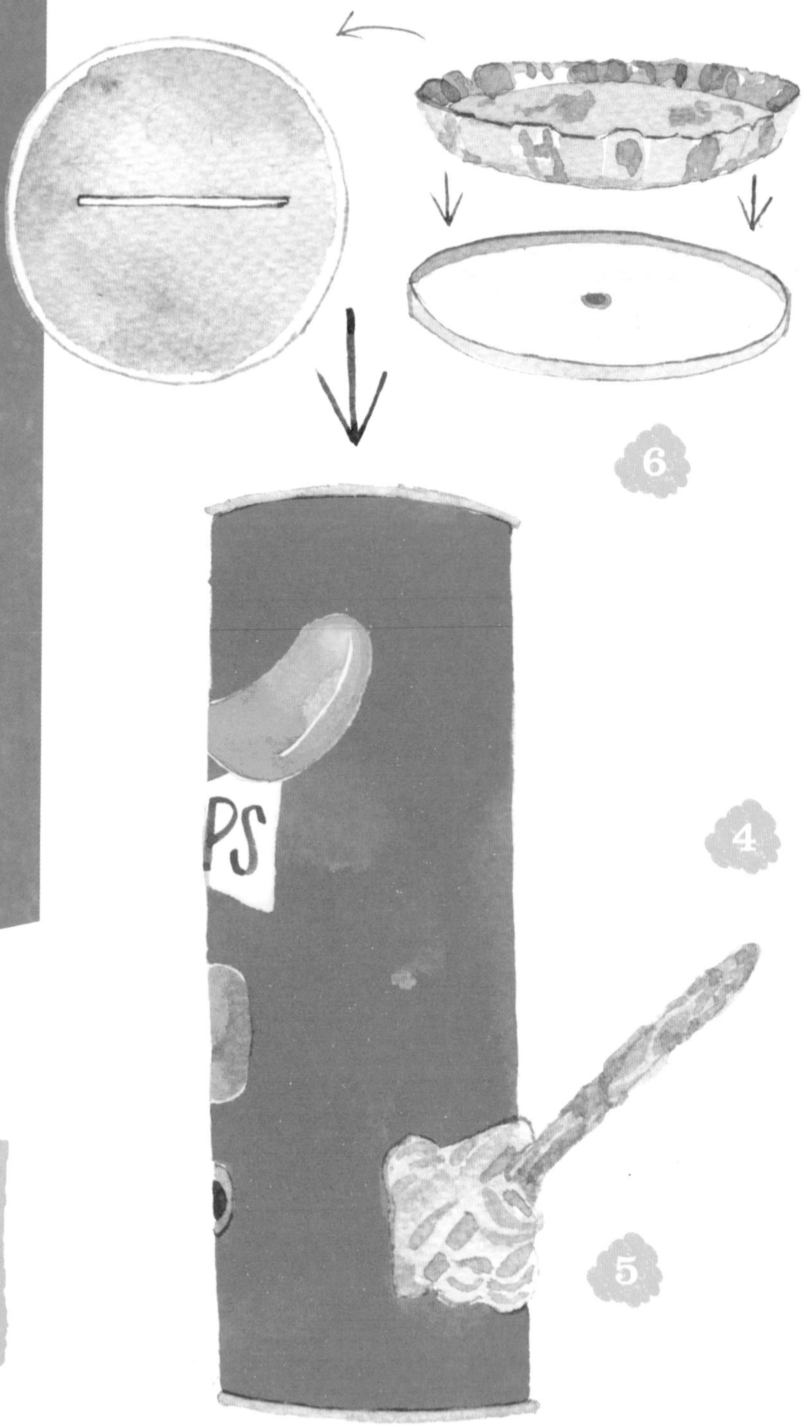
6
PS
4
5

How is the light that you see **with** the spectroscope different from the light when you look at the light source **without** the spectroscope?

What might this tell you about the **light** coming from the thing you're looking at?

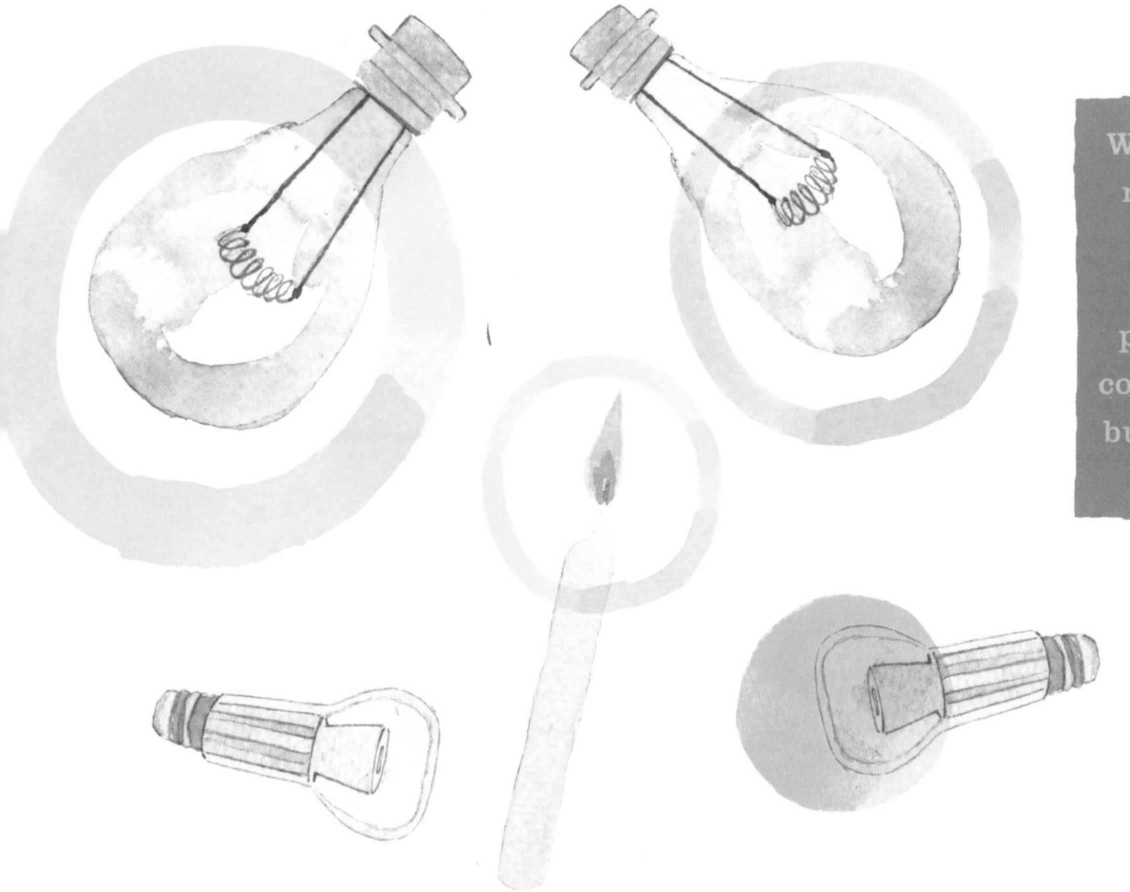

What **differences** do you notice when you point the spectroscope at different light sources? (It's particularly interesting to compare energy-saving light bulbs with fluorescent tubes or filament bulbs.)

MR SHAHA says...

White light, like that from the sun, is a mixture of different colours of light. The surface of the CD is marked with thousands of tiny lines, so it is not like an ordinary mirror. These lines make different colours of light bounce off at slightly different angles, so when white light is reflected from the CD, the different colours of light separate out to form a spectrum. Something similar happens when light from the sun passes through raindrops and forms a rainbow.

Although you can see a spectrum by just holding up a CD to the light, the design of the spectroscope allows us to keep out stray light and look at a specific light source to see its constituent colours. Spectroscopes are very useful to scientists – different elements, like hydrogen, helium, and lithium, give out different colours of light, so looking at stars through a spectroscope lets astronomers learn about their composition.

THE TELEKINETIC STRAW

Some magicians claim to be able to perform 'telekinesis' – making objects move by just thinking about moving them. This activity will literally let you move objects without touching them, and do other things that look like genuine wizardry. It may not be real magic, but this activity will introduce you to the forces associated with 'static' electricity and its similarities to magnetism.

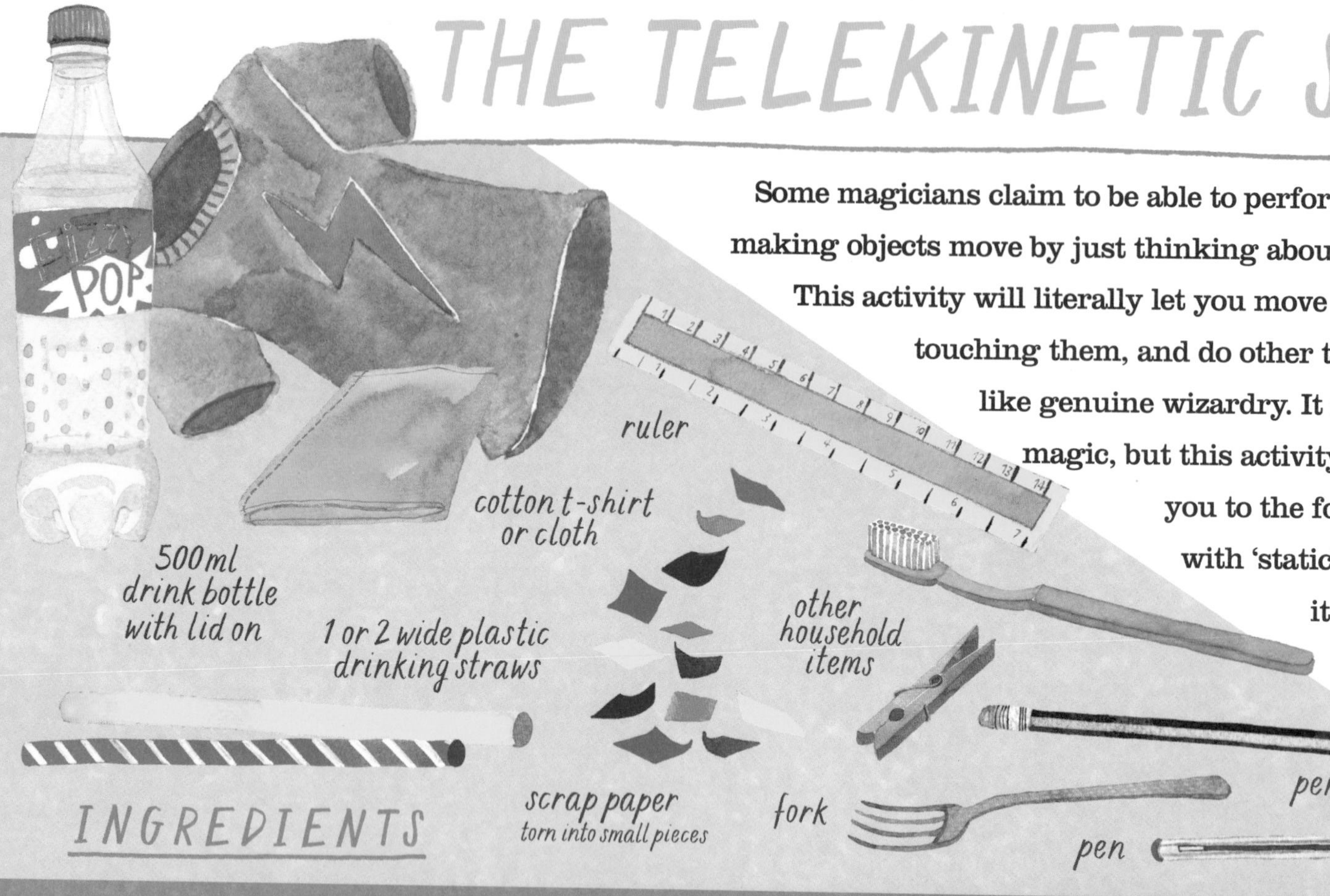

FIZZY POP
ruler
cotton t-shirt or cloth
500ml drink bottle with lid on
1 or 2 wide plastic drinking straws
other household items
scrap paper torn into small pieces
fork
pencil
pen

INGREDIENTS

METHOD

1 It could be fun to perform this experiment as a magic trick.

2 Place the straw on top of the bottle and immediately take it off as if you've noticed it's dirty. Give it a good rub with your t-shirt as if you're cleaning it, then place it back on top of the bottle. At this point, you may find that the straw sticks to your fingers, so you may need to practise placing it on the bottle in a way that doesn't give the trick away.

3 Once you've balanced the straw on the bottle lid, bring your hand close to the end of the straw that you rubbed. The straw should start moving towards you, even though you haven't touched it. You can revel in your magic skills for a short time before explaining that the secret to making the straw move like this is in 'charging' it up by rubbing it. Then try some of the variations on the next page.

use the power!

? How **close** do you have to bring your hand before the straw starts to move?

? Does it matter how much you **rub** the straw before putting it on the bottle?

Rip up some scrap paper into tiny pieces and scatter them on the table. 'Charge up' a straw and bring it close to the bits of paper.

Does how much you rub the straw affect how much paper it will pick up?

Try doing the experiment with two straws. Charge one up and balance it on the bottle. Charge up the second straw then bring it close to the straw on the bottle.

FIZZY
POP

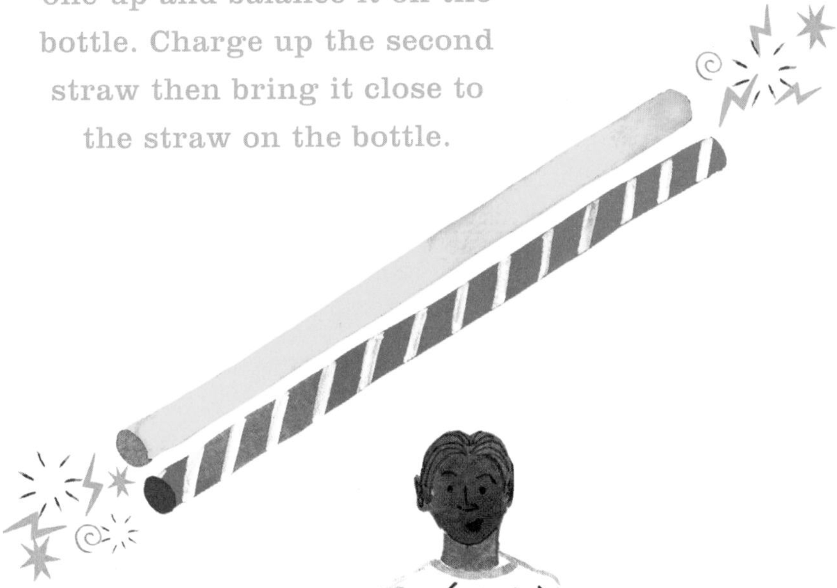

Do you think the straw will move if you use another object instead of your hand? Does the straw behave differently with different objects?

Turn on a tap so that it produces a steady trickle of water. 'Charge up' a straw and bring it close to the water. **What do you think will happen?**

MR SHAHA says...

Everything contains electric charge, a mixture of **positive** and **negative**. Normally these cancel each other out. But when we rub the straw with the t-shirt, some of the negative charge from the cloth rubs off on the straw. The straw gains a negative charge and the t-shirt is left with a positive charge.

wheee
RUBBING
*friction

As you rub, tiny particles called electrons are rubbed off the t-shirt onto the straw. Electrons are very, very tiny, much tinier than the atoms that make up everything. Each electron has a negative charge and that's why the straw becomes negatively charged.

When things are 'charged up' in this way with 'static' electricity, they may attract or repel other things. This is similar to, but not the same as, the way that magnets can attract or repel other things.

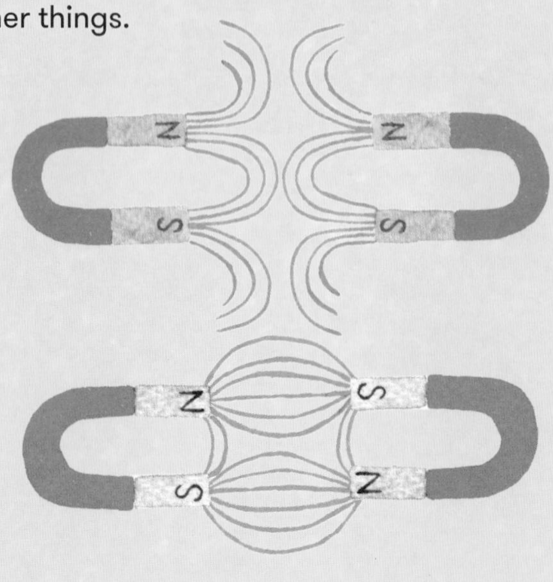
N
S
N
S
N
S
S
N

If two things have **opposite** charges, they attract, or pull towards each other.

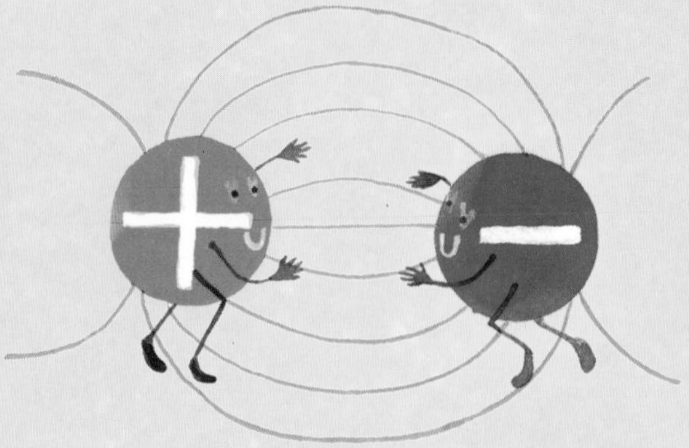

If two things have the **same** charge, they repel, or push away from each other. This is why two charged up straws repel each other.

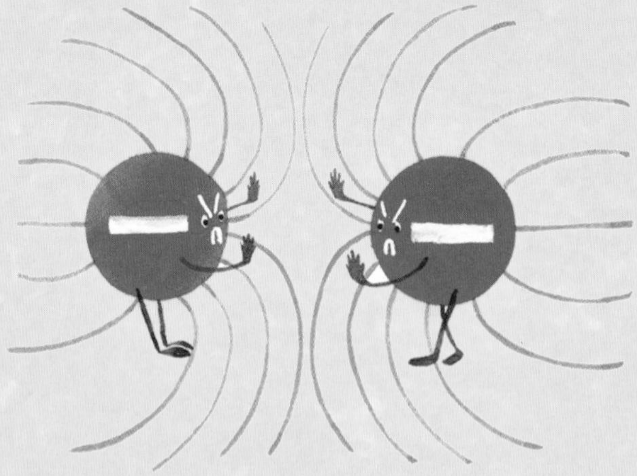

A charged straw is attracted to your hand because the straw has a negative charge and there are positive charges in your hand. The same is true of water, pencils, and other objects that are attracted towards the straw.

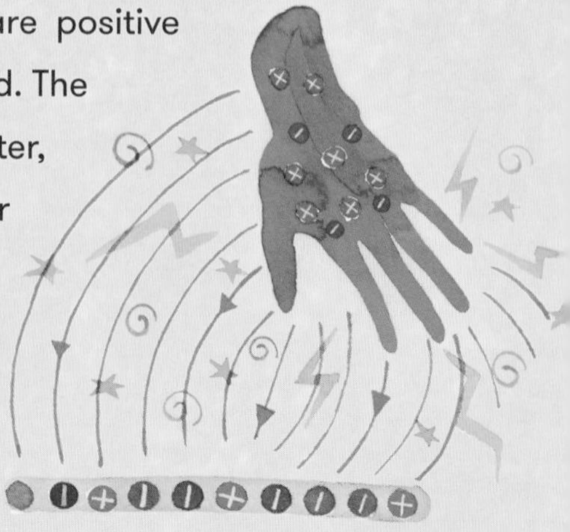

ATOMS

OCO
OCO
OCO
OCO

One of the most popular toys in the world is Lego. So many of the little interlocking plastic bricks have been produced that, if divided equally, everyone on the planet could have almost a hundred pieces each.

Part of the charm of Lego is that anything you make with it can be taken apart so that you can make something new. Remarkably, this is very much like the way the natural world is constructed – everything in the world is made of building blocks called atoms and, although it may not be obvious in everyday life, these can be taken apart from each other and rearranged to make new substances.

This is what happens when ice melts into water, when the ingredients in a cake are cooked, when plants take carbon dioxide in from the air and give out oxygen, and in countless other processes that are going on all around us. The following activities produce wondrous results, which can be explained using the 'atomic hypothesis' – the idea that everything is made up of particles.

the ACIDS
THE ALKALINES

MICROSCOPIC MOVEMENT

We can't see atoms because they are much too small. If you took an apple and made it as big as the Earth, the atoms in it would be about as big as the original apple. Sadly, we can't do this, but we don't have to see atoms to know they exist – instead, we can observe them indirectly. This activity shows us something that is the result of the way atoms behave.

cold water from the fridge
3 identical glasses or jars
room temperature water
thermometer (optional)
liquid food colouring
hot tap water
dropper (optional)

INGREDIENTS

1 Hr
1

METHOD

1 Before doing this activity, fill two of the glasses or jars with roughly the same amount of water. Put one in the fridge and leave one out so that it reaches room temperature.

2 Once you're ready to start, get one more glass and fill it with hot water from the tap, making sure you use the same amount of water as in the other glasses.

3 Carefully put a few drops of food colouring into the water at room temperature and see what happens.

20°c

2

? Why is it important to use the same amount of water? How could you make sure you're using the same amount of water in each case?

3
ROOM
COLD
HOT

What do you think will happen if you put food colouring into the **cold** or **hot** water? Try both.

What do you think this activity might tell you about how **temperature** affects water particles?

MR SHAHA says…

Using the same amounts, and the same type of glass or jar, helps make the experiments in this activity a 'fair test'. The main difference between the cold, warm and hot water is temperature. In everyday life, knowing the temperature of something can be useful – so that we don't burn ourselves by touching something hot, for example. The scientific definition of temperature is related to the speed at which the particles in a substance are moving: the higher the temperature, the faster the particles move.

SOLID
GAS
LIQUID

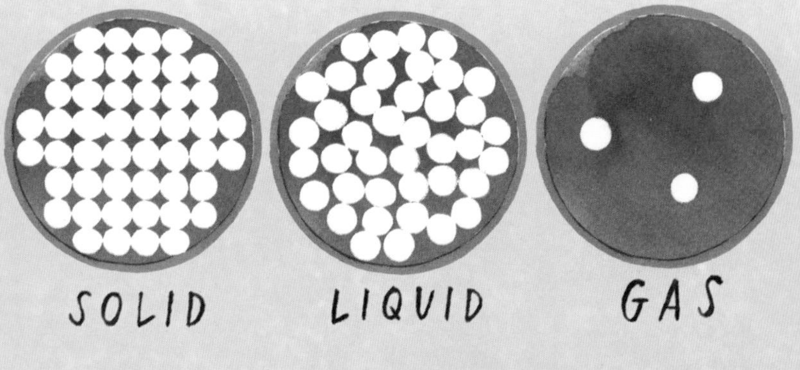
SOLID
LIQUID
GAS

Atoms in solids, liquids and gases are always moving; the more energy they have, the more they move. When we put food colouring into the hot water, it changes colour more quickly than in the cooler water because the particles are moving around faster, which means they spread the particles of food colouring around more quickly.

CRAZY QUICK CUPCAKES

Changing one thing into another might seem like magic, but there's an everyday activity where we do just that: cooking. I love how things that you wouldn't eat as they are, like flour and lentils, can be transformed into delicious things, like roti and dal. Cooking isn't just *like* chemistry, it often really *is* chemistry. Many of the processes that change raw ingredients into food we want to eat are chemical reactions, and this activity is a delicious way to see that for yourself.

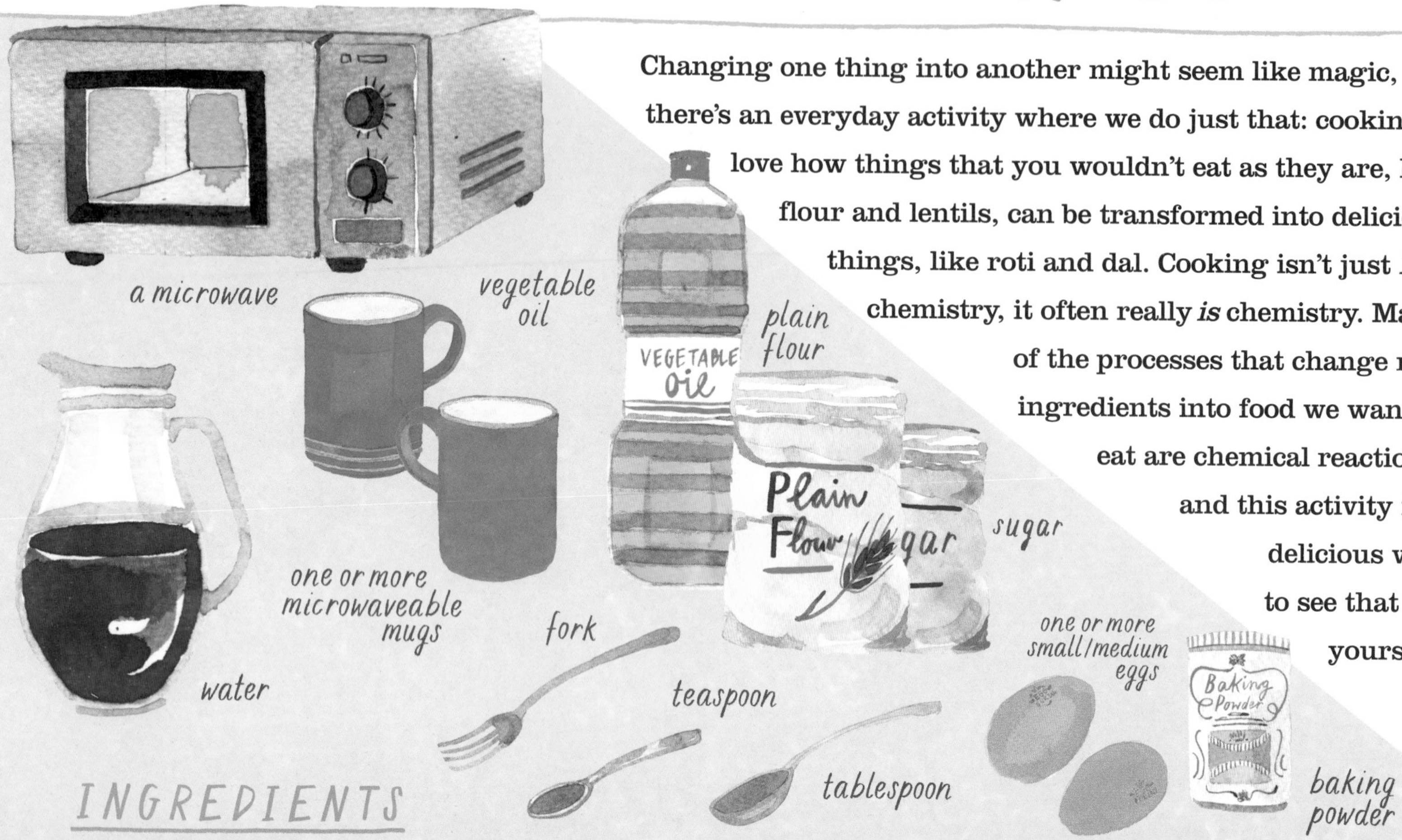
a microwave
vegetable oil
VEGETABLE Oil
plain flour
Plain Flour
sugar
one or more microwaveable mugs
fork
water
teaspoon
one or more small/medium eggs
Baking Powder
tablespoon
baking powder

INGREDIENTS

METHOD

1 Put these ingredients into a mug:

- 4 tablespoons plain flour
- 2 tablespoons caster sugar
- 1/4 teaspoon baking powder
- 1 small/medium egg
- 2 tablespoons vegetable oil
- 2 tablespoons water

2 Stir thoroughly using a fork. Make sure there are no lumps of flour left at the bottom.

? What does the batter **look/feel/ taste** like?
What do we need to do to turn this into a **cake?**

3 Cook the mixture in the microwave on full power for 2 minutes.

! **4** Remove and allow to cool.

You can eat the cake straight out of the mug, but if you want to examine it closely, you can put it onto a plate.

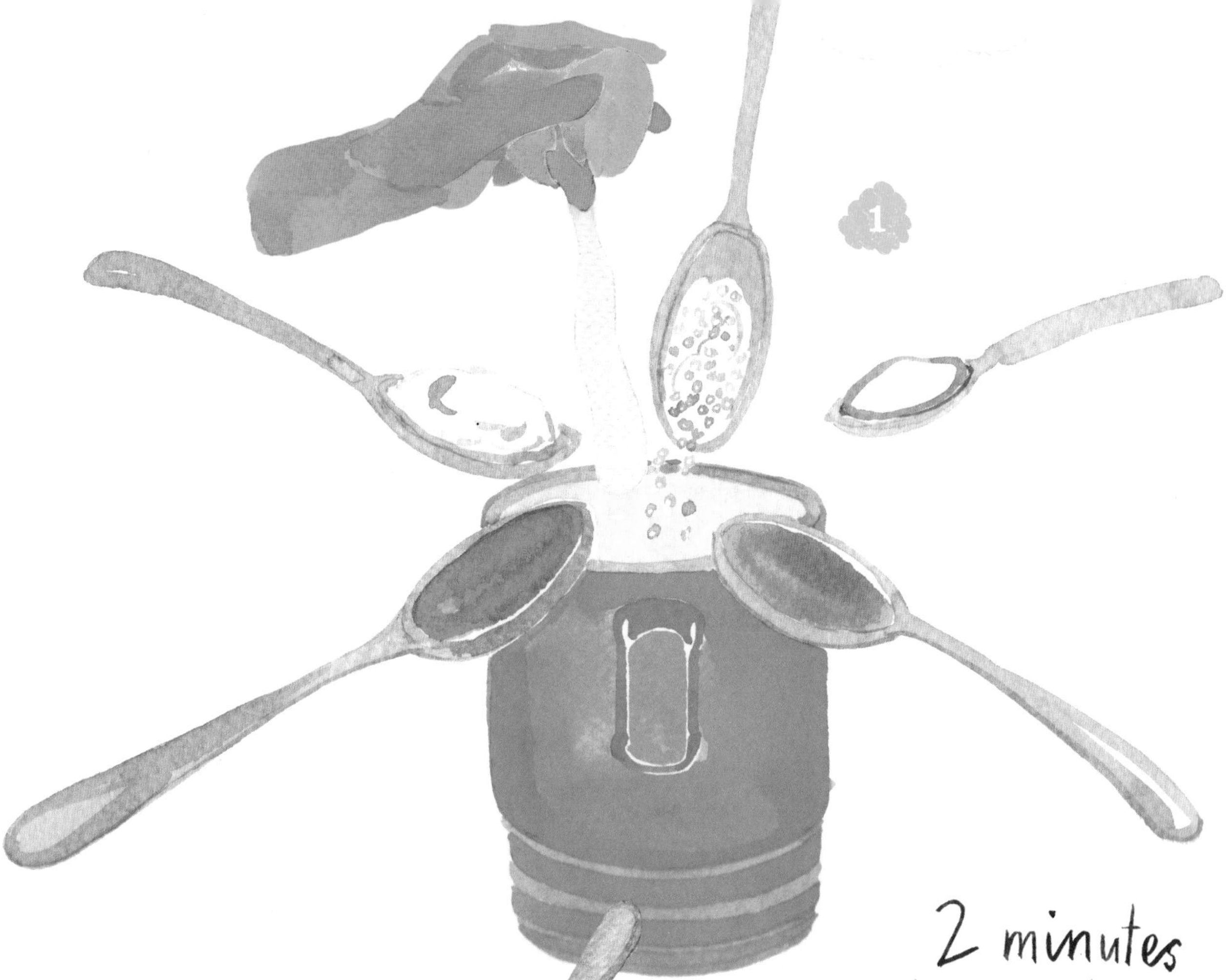
1

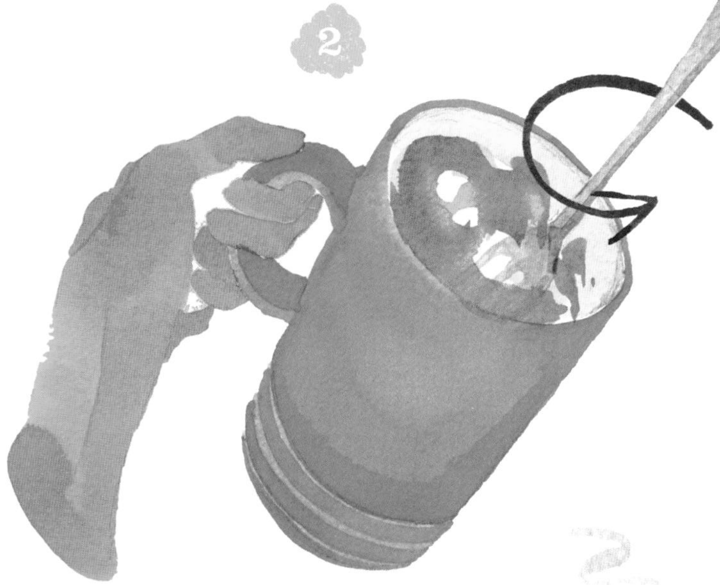
2

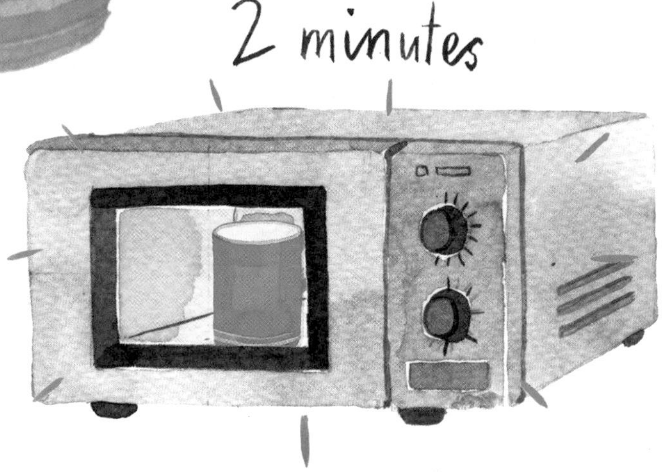
2 minutes
3

4

BE SAFE

? What does the cake look/ feel/taste like now?

What do you think will happen if you cook the cake mixture without **egg** or without **oil?**

If you've got enough ingredients, you could try leaving out other ingredients, one at a time. Which is the **tastiest** cake?!

yum!
LEANING TOWER OF CAKE
PAN-CAKE
GOBI DESSERT
SPECTRUMENDOUS

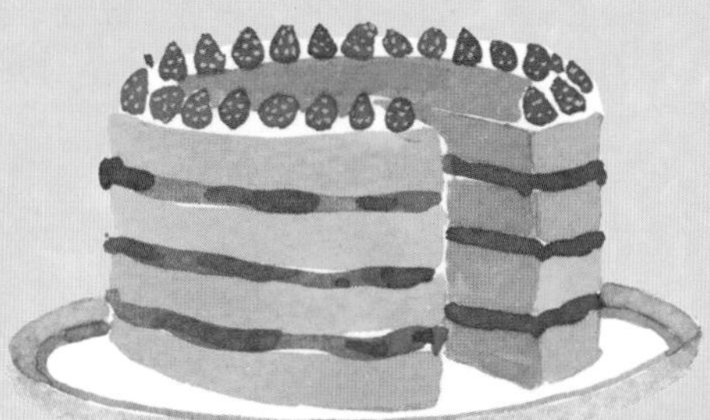

yum!
yum!

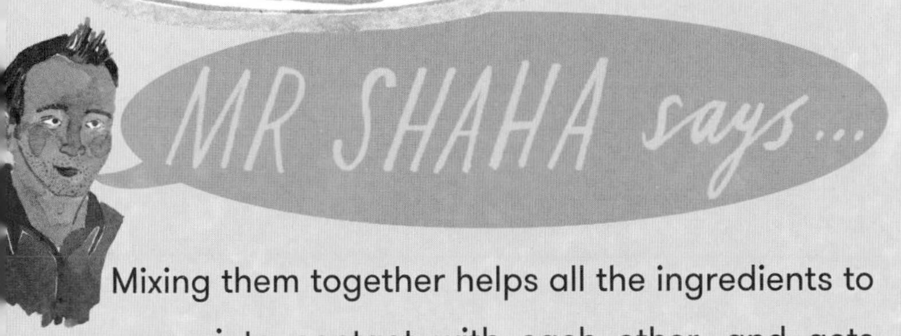
MR SHAHA says...

Mixing them together helps all the ingredients to come into contact with each other, and gets them ready to react with each other.

FLOUR
FLOUR
SUGAR
SUGAR
EGG
BAKING POWDER
WATER
OIL
FLOUR
OIL
WATER

The microwave provides the energy needed for the chemical reactions to take place and turn the mixture into cake.

The oil coats all the other ingredients. If you don't include it in your cake, the other ingredients dry out when heated, leaving you with a dry cake. Baking powder contains chemicals that react to produce carbon dioxide gas when the cake is cooking. This gas gets trapped in little pockets in the cake, and makes it spongy. Leaving out baking powder means you'll get a flat cake.

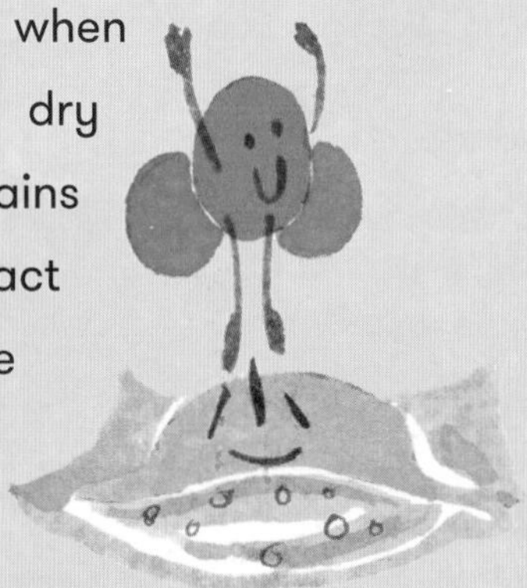

Leaving out the egg produces a cake that doesn't have much structure. That's because eggs contain long chain-like molecules (called proteins) which unravel and form new hard, strong structures inside the cake when cooked (similar to when you fry or boil an egg).

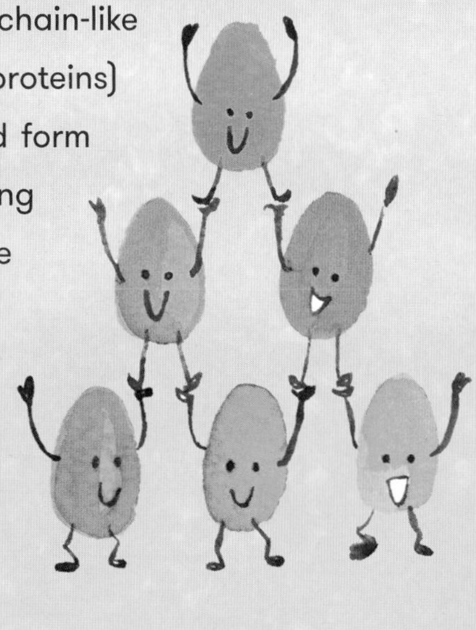

BALLOON-INFLATION MACHINE

Science and technology are closely related. Scientists find out new things about the world, and new technologies often use that knowledge to make our lives easier. Blowing up a balloon is hard work, but this activity uses the science of chemistry to let you make a balloon-inflating machine that does the work for you.

INGREDIENTS

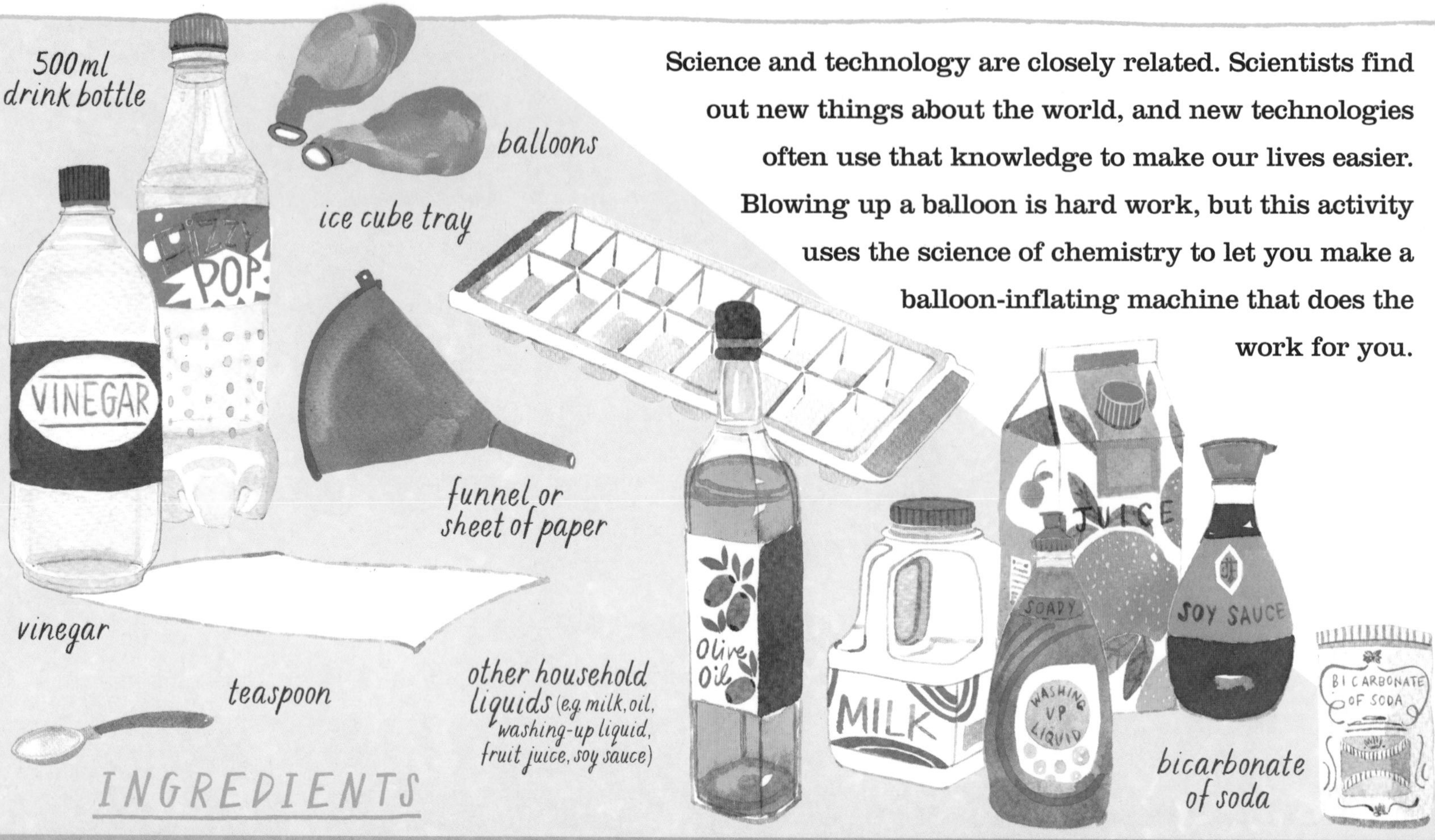
500ml drink bottle
balloons
ice cube tray
VINEGAR
POP
funnel or sheet of paper
vinegar
teaspoon
other household liquids (e.g. milk, oil, washing-up liquid, fruit juice, soy sauce)
Olive Oil
MILK
JUICE
SOAPY
WASHING UP LIQUID
SOY SAUCE
BICARBONATE OF SODA
bicarbonate of soda

METHOD

PART ONE

1 Prepare an ice cube tray so that each compartment is about half-filled with a different household liquid.

2 Spoon a little bicarbonate into one of the compartments. What happens? Repeat this with each of the liquids in the ice cube tray, trying to make it a fair test by adding the same amount of bicarbonate to each.

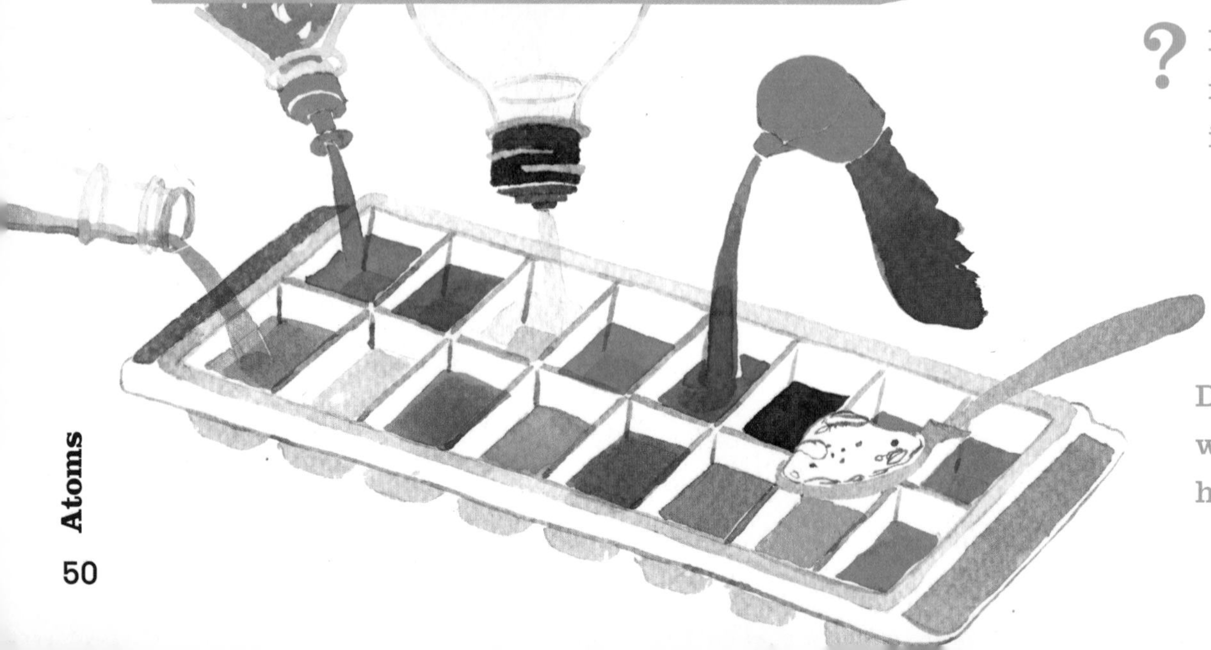

? If there are any bubbles formed, what do you think is **inside** the bubbles?

Which liquid produced the **most** bubbles?

Do the liquids that **fizz** with the bicarbonate of soda have anything in common?

PART TWO

1 Prepare your balloon by stretching it.

2 Fill 1/3 of the bottle with vinegar.

3 Use a funnel, or a rolled up sheet of paper, to spoon bicarbonate into the balloon until the round part is 1/2 full.

4 Stretch the mouth of the balloon over the open end of the bottle, taking care not to spill any of the bicarbonate into the vinegar.

5 To inflate the balloon, hold it up so the bicarbonate falls into the vinegar.

1
3
1/2
FULL
POP
4

What happens if you add **more** bicarbonate of soda?

MR SHAHA says...

Sometimes, when we combine two or more substances, they react with each other to make a new substance. This is called a chemical reaction. When bicarbonate is added to some liquids, it reacts with the liquid and produces carbon dioxide gas (also known as CO_2).

The fizzing we see and hear is caused by the carbon dioxide making bubbles in the liquid as it escapes, a bit like when you blow through a straw into a drink.

VINEGAR
BICARBONATE soda
OCO
OCO
OCO
OCO
OCO

The bicarbonate does not react with all liquids. You might notice that the liquids it does react with have something in common: they all tend to be sour or 'sharp' tasting. These liquids, like vinegar, are what scientists call acidic.

In this experiment, the gas produced when the bicarbonate reacts with vinegar is trapped in the balloon. This is similar to the way in which bicarbonate is used in cooking – the gas it produces when it reacts is trapped inside pockets of bread or cake, which makes them spongy and nice to eat.

COLOUR-CHANGING CABBAGE

Things in the natural world often have properties that we cannot detect with our own senses, but science lets us overcome this limitation. If you've ever had a blood test, you'll know that scientists can carry out analysis of substances to tell us everything from whether we have a particular disease to whether we're eating properly. By making use of a surprising property of an everyday food, this activity allows you to do some basic chemical analysis at home.

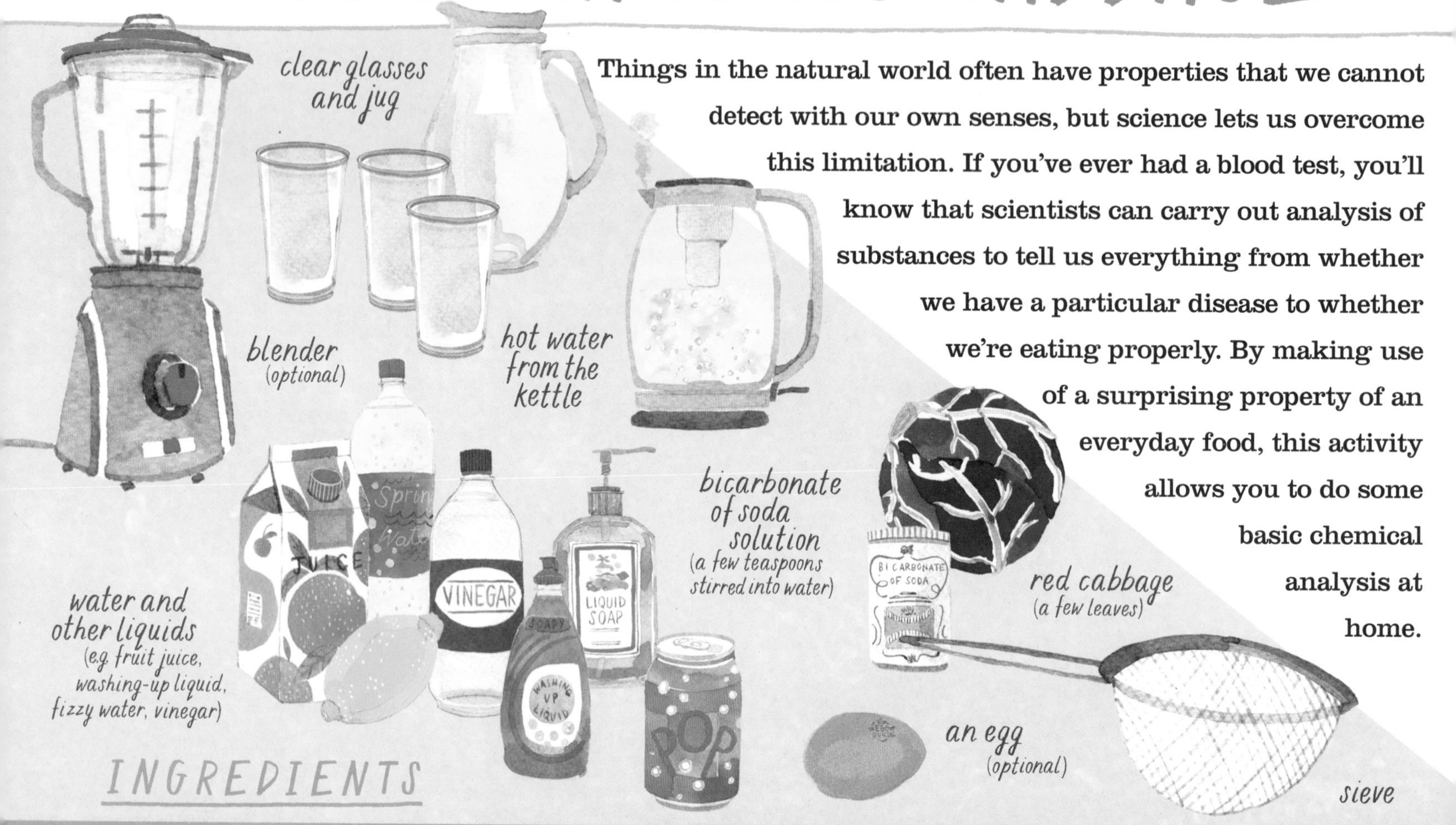
clear glasses and jug
blender (optional)
hot water from the kettle
bicarbonate of soda solution (a few teaspoons stirred into water)
red cabbage (a few leaves)
water and other liquids (e.g. fruit juice, washing-up liquid, fizzy water, vinegar)
JUICE
VINEGAR
LIQUID SOAP
SOAPY
WASHING UP LIQUID
BI CARBONATE OF SODA
POP
an egg (optional)
sieve

INGREDIENTS

METHOD

1 If you **have** a blender, place a handful of chopped or torn up raw cabbage leaves into it. Add some cold water to cover. Blitz the cabbage and water together until you can see that the water has gone dark purple. Pour the contents of the blender into a jug through a sieve so that you separate any remaining bits of cabbage leaves from the purple liquid. Add the same amount of water to the purple liquid, so you get twice the amount of liquid in your jug. Now you're ready to experiment.

If you **don't have** a blender, chop or tear up the cabbage leaves into small pieces and soak them in boiling-hot water. Wait for the liquid to cool, then use it as described below.

2 Pour a little bit of this purple liquid into a glass (1/2 full at most).

3 Slowly pour a little bit of vinegar into the purple liquid. Add more if there is not an immediate or obvious change.

4 Repeat this with other liquids, testing to see what effect they have on the cabbage juice, using a new glass each time.

5 Try an egg or the bicarbonate of soda solution if you have some.

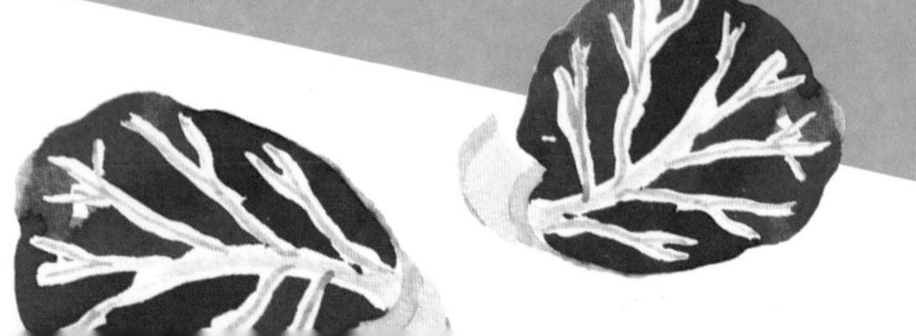

BE SAFE
1 (with a blender)
1 (without a blender)

3
4
LIQUID SOAP

? What do you notice about the liquids that make the cabbage juice turn **red** and those that make the cabbage juice turn **blue** or **green**? Do they have anything in common?

Once you've identified liquids that make the cabbage juice go red or blue, see what happens when you **mix** them. Is it possible to get the cabbage juice back to its original colour?

Try to make a **rainbow** of glasses using cabbage juice with different substances put in it.

MR SHAHA says...

When you put cabbage in water, some of the chemicals that make it red (or purple) dissolve in the water. These chemicals are called anthocyanins. Blitzing the cabbage, or soaking it in hot water, are simple ways to extract these chemicals.

the ACIDS

When the cabbage juice is mixed with different liquids, it changes colour because a chemical reaction takes place. The colour change we see depends on the properties of the liquid we test. We call liquids like cabbage juice 'indicator solutions', because they tell us something about the chemical composition of other substances.

THE ALKALINES

In this case, substances that make the cabbage juice go red have properties that scientists categorise as acidic, and ones that make the cabbage juice go blue or green are known as alkaline. At home, substances that taste sharp, like orange juice and vinegar, tend to be acidic.

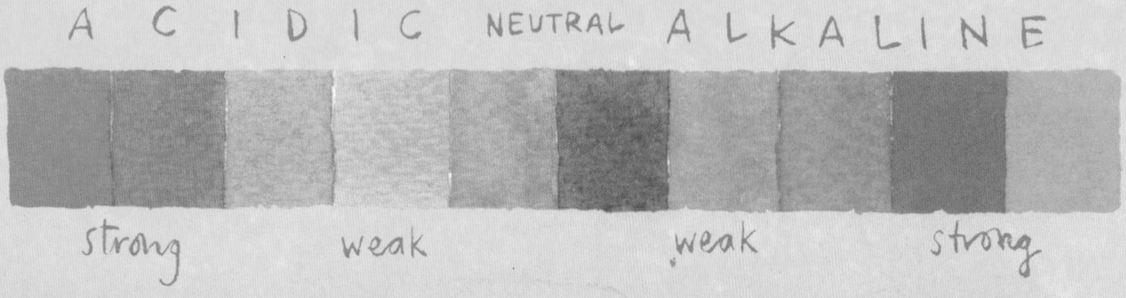

ACIDIC
NEUTRAL
ALKALINE
strong
weak
weak
strong

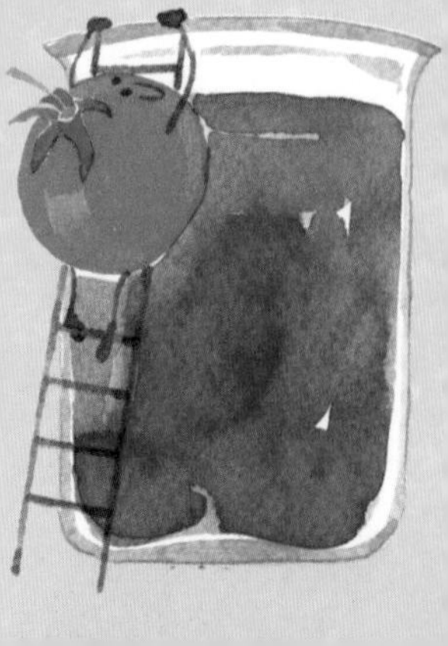

LIVING THINGS

As I write this, scientists all over the world are excited about the discovery of a planet orbiting the star Proxima Centauri, the closest star to our own sun. Other planets have been discovered outside the solar system, but 'Proxima b' has properties that suggest it could support life. However, it's unlikely that we'll find anything like the richness and diversity of life here on Earth.

Our home planet is the only one in the solar system, and perhaps even in the whole universe, where life has flourished. There might be a bacteria or two in some crevice on Mars or primitive underwater organisms beneath the seas of Jupiter's moon Europa, but all the evidence we have at the moment suggests that the complex, highly evolved life on earth is unique. Life elsewhere might be unlike anything we can imagine, but scientists are confident they'll recognise evidence for it, if and when they find it.

Learning about living things presents scientists with challenges that are different to studying, say, chemical reactions or physical processes. I've chosen the following activities to demonstrate some of the fascinating things scientists have found out about life and how it works.

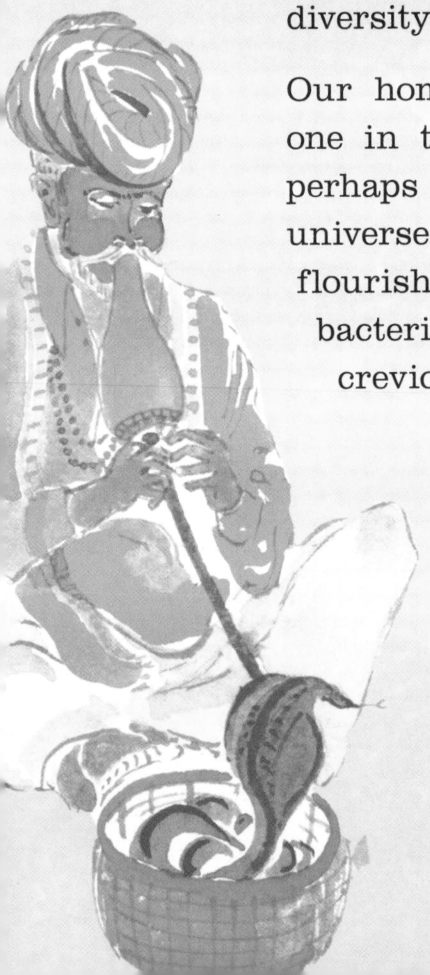

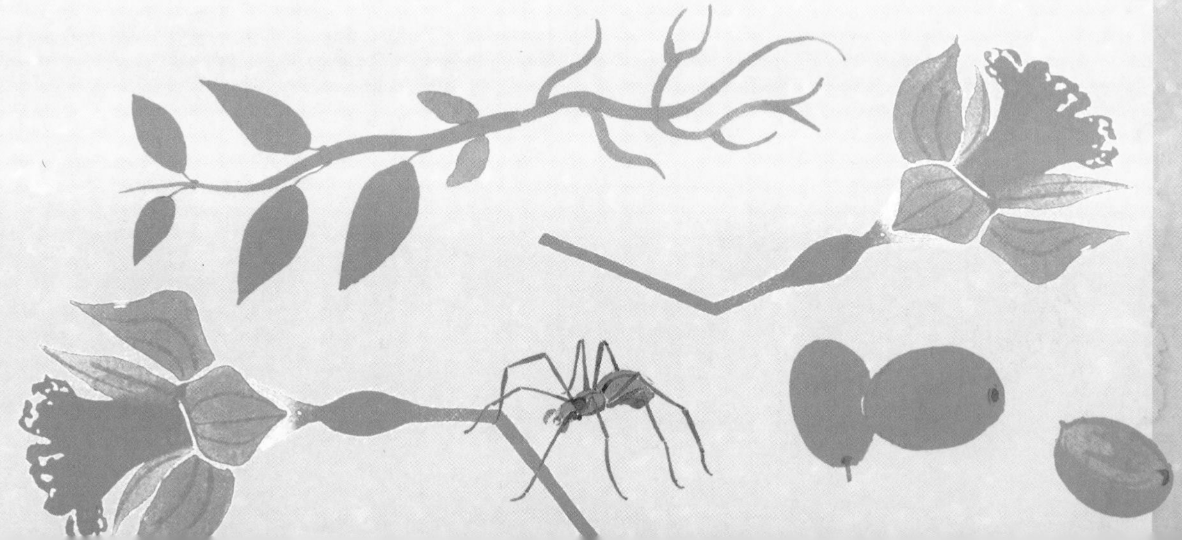

DAFFODIL DISSECTION

one or more flowers
scissors or tweezers
(optional)

INGREDIENTS

Flowers are among the most beautiful living things in nature, and they produce seeds and fruit that many animals rely upon for food. Both these things are related to the role a flower has in the life of a plant – to help it reproduce.

We usually look at the outside of flowers, but this activity involves looking inside them because sometimes, to learn about how something works, we need to open it up to look more closely.

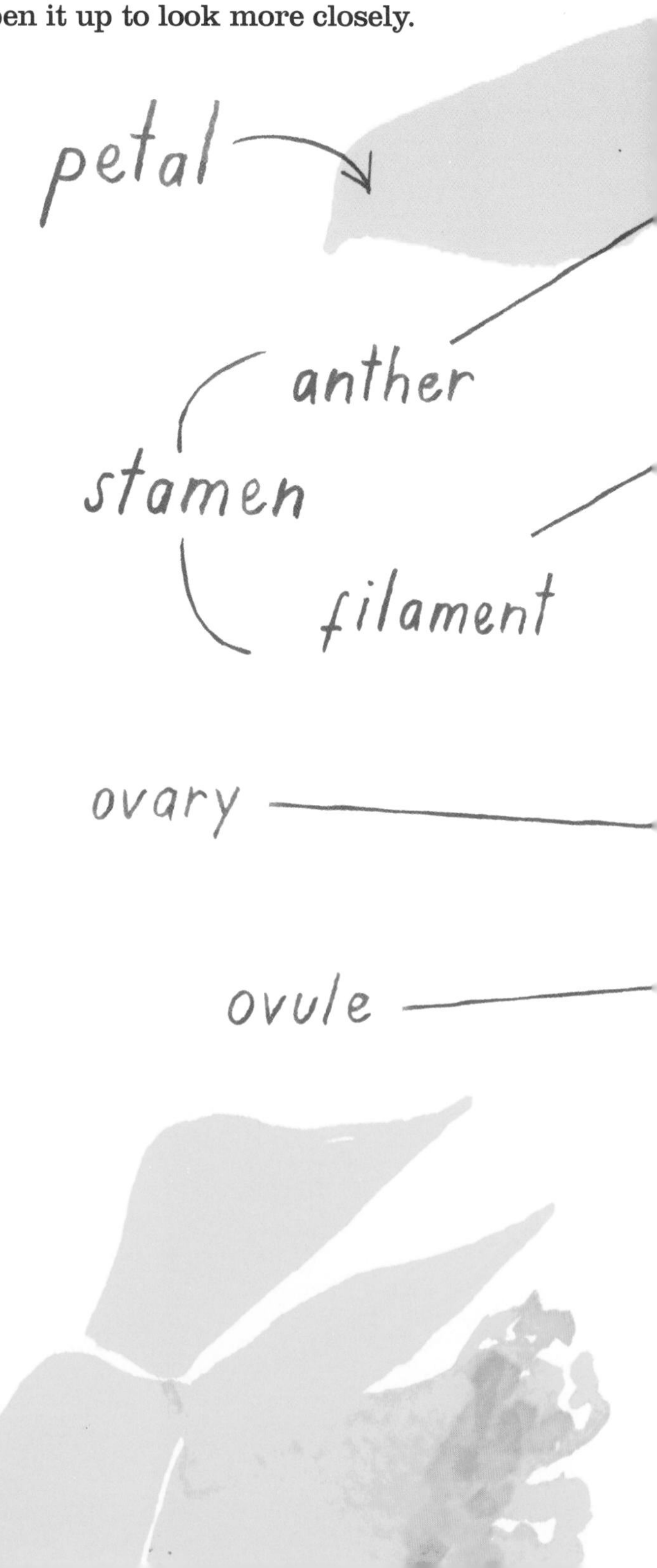

petal
anther
stamen
filament
ovary
ovule

METHOD

1 Take a look at the main picture – Emily has made a diagram of a flower that she found. This is a simplified drawing showing the individual features that most flowers have.

2 Now choose your own flower and, using your fingers or the tweezers, carefully take the petals away from one side to reveal what's underneath. Then examine it closely.

3 Try to draw your flower and label any features you recognise from Emily's diagram.

4 Next, see if you can separate out each part of the flower and study each one. You can learn more about the purpose of each part by reading **Mr Shaha Says**.

? In which ways is your flower **similar** to Emily's flower? How is it **different?**

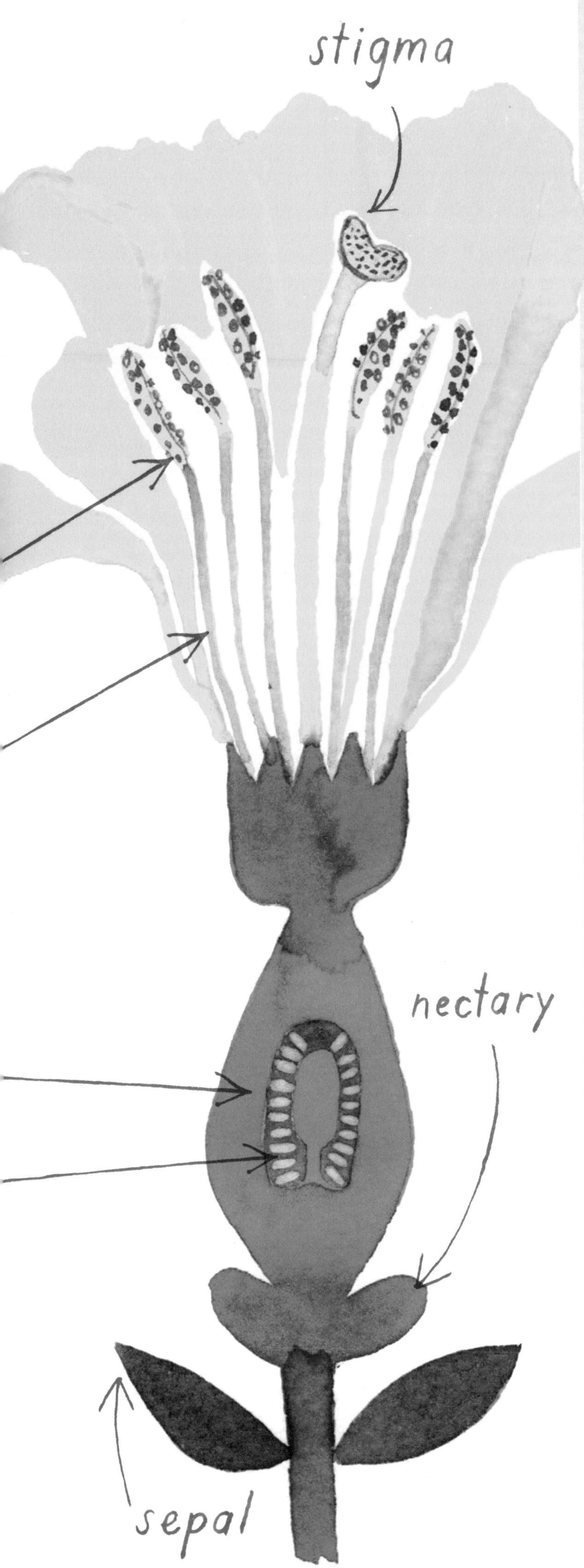
stigma
nectary
sepal

MR SHAHA says...

There are countless varieties of flowers out there, in all sorts of shapes and sizes, but most of them have the structures shown in the diagram. Each part has a different role to play in helping the plant to reproduce:

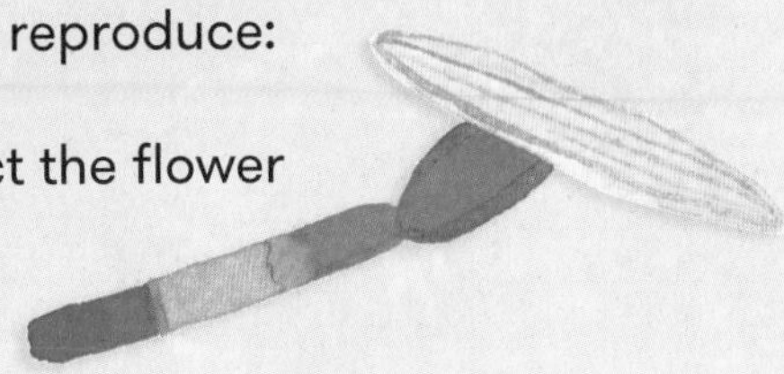

Sepals These protect the flower before it has opened.

Petals These protect the inside of the flower and may be brightly coloured to attract insects and other animals.

Stamens
These are made up of a **filament** holding up an **anther**, where the pollen grains (male sex cells) are made.

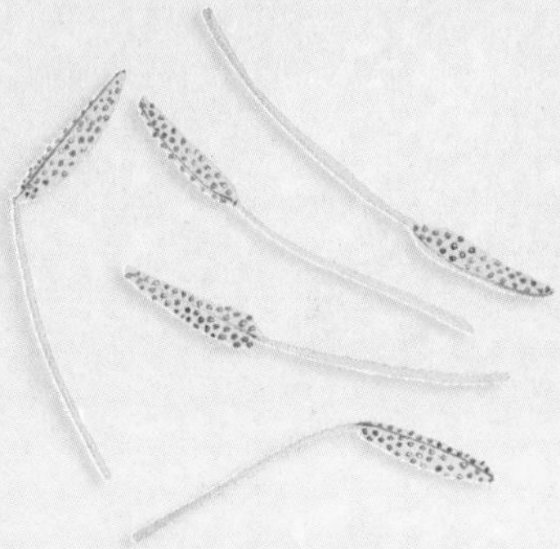

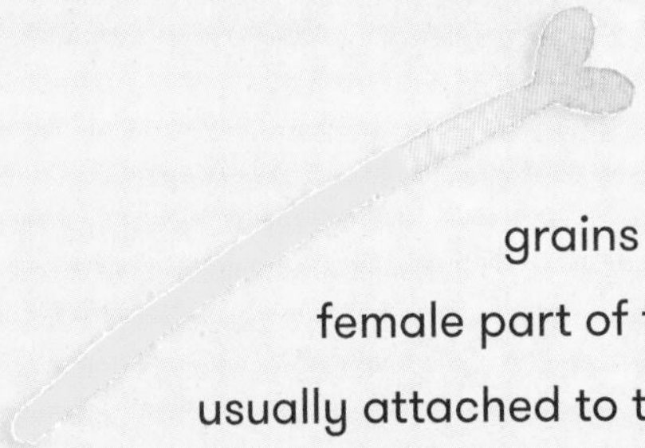

Stigma
This is where pollen grains are collected by the female part of the flower. These are usually attached to the ovary by a **style**.

Ovary
This contains ovules, which contain eggs (the female sex cells).

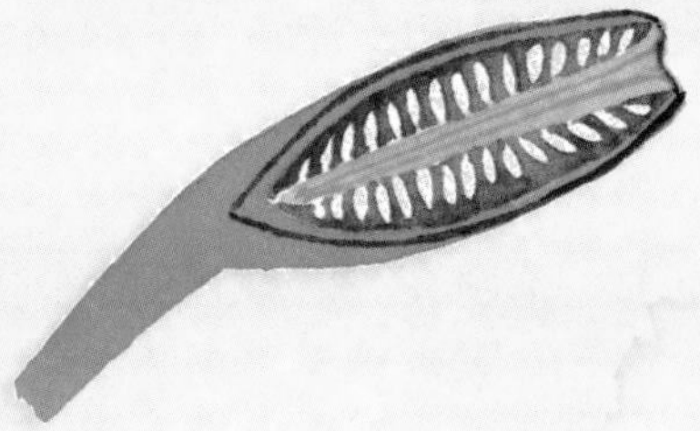

Nectary This is where nectar, a sugary solution that attracts insects, is produced.

DEAD OR ALIVE

MY WONDER JOURNAL

INGREDIENTS

- paper
- pen or pencil
- the pictures from page 59

How can you tell if something is alive or not? You may feel that you can 'just tell', but scientists need to have accurate ways of testing for the presence or absence of life. Being able to define whether something is living or not can be useful for all sorts of reasons, from deciding whether we've discovered life on other planets to recognising when computers or other human-made things should be considered 'alive'. This activity gets you thinking about one of the most important questions in science.

METHOD

1 On a piece of paper, write down the heading **Characteristics of Living Things**.

2 Look at the pictures on the opposite page and pick any three things from the side that has living things and three things from the side that has non-living things.

3 Think about how you knew which things were living and which were not.

4 On your piece of paper, write down all the features that the living things have in common but the non-living things don't. For example, some of the things pictured can move on their own and some of them can't, so you might write 'can move by itself' as a characteristic.

5 Repeat this with three more living and non-living things, but try to find characteristics that you haven't already used.

6 Repeat this again so that you have now used all the pictures.

? Look at your list of characteristics. Is there any one characteristic that **only** living things have?

If so, do you think that one characteristic could **always** be used to tell whether something is a living thing or not?

If not, what do you think is the **minimum** number of characteristics that would confirm that it was a living thing? What characteristics are they?

NON-LIVING
LIVING

LIVING
NON-LIVING
tree
wind-up toy mouse
young girl
HELLO
computer
mushroom
fire
bacteria
star
mule (cannot have babies)
book
old person
water
hibernating bear
rock
spider
sausages
seedless grape
tornado

MR SHAHA says...

As you may have found out from doing this activity, there is no single property that is common to all living things and no single test to determine whether something is alive, was once alive, or never lived at all. It might surprise you, but the apparently simple question 'what is life?' is a controversial one in science because we have yet to agree on a definitive answer. It may even be that living and non-living are not two completely distinct categories.

PARP!

For most purposes, we can use the following characteristics, which you can remember using the acronym *MRS GREN*

Movement – all living things can move by themselves, even plants, which turn to point at the sun.

Respiration – this is the chemical process by which living things obtain energy from food.

Sensitivity – all living things have the ability to detect and respond to changes in their environment.

Growth – all living things get bigger or develop in other ways as they get older.

Reproduction – all living things can make more living things that are the same type as them.

Excretion – all living things produce and get rid of waste products.

Nutrition – all living things need food to stay alive.

GERMINATION IN A JAR

water
paper towels
one or more seeds (pea or bean work very well)
glass or jar

INGREDIENTS

Deep inside a snow-covered mountain on an island in the Arctic North, there is a 'disaster-proof' bank. It contains seeds from thousands of plant species around the world, which may help us rebuild civilisation in the event of an apocalypse. Seeds have always struck me as remarkable: they contain the basic ingredients and 'instructions' to grow everything from a tiny blade of grass to a giant tree. This activity allows you to see for yourself the amazing process by which a plant emerges from a seed.

METHOD

1 Scrunch up some paper towels and pack them into the glass or jar.

2 Slowly pour some water into the jar to make the paper towels damp.

3 Press down on the paper to squeeze out any excess water and pour it away – the paper should not be soaking wet. Add more paper towels to the jar if necessary and make this wet too.

4 Use a finger to push a seed down the side of the glass so that it is pressed against the side of the glass by the paper, about 1/2 to 1/3 of the way down. (If you find this difficult, you can use something like a pencil or chopstick.)

2

3
4
5
SEED
1
BEANS

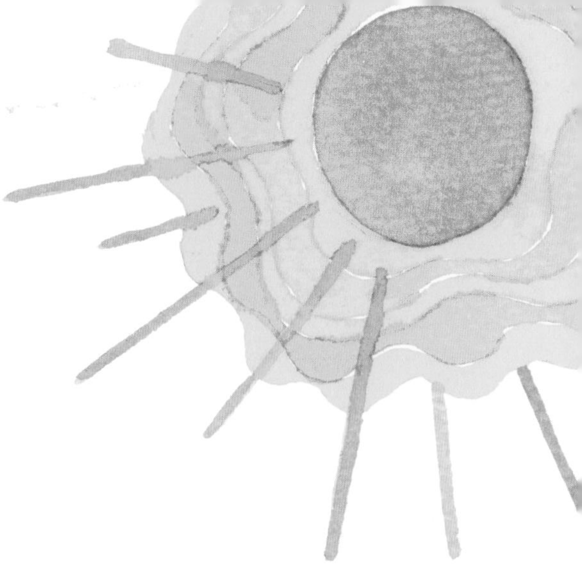

5 If you have more than one seed, you can put up to four of them around the glass. If you're using more than one type of seed, for example a pea seed and a bean seed, you should label the glass so you know which is which when they grow over the next few days.

6 Leave the glass in a sunny place and wait – you should see changes in the next day or so. Pour more water into the towels if they seem very dry over the next few days.

7 Record what happens to your seeds (Hint: use your artistic talents...).

? If you're using different types of seed, which do you think will sprout **first?** Why?

PEA
SEEDS
SEED 1
SEED 2
DAY 1
DAY 2

What do you think would happen if you used **dry** kitchen towels instead of wet ones? Why?

JAM
JAM
SEEDS
JUICE

What do you think would happen if you put the jar in a **dark** cupboard?

Do you think it makes a difference if the seeds are **hot** or **cold?** How could you find out?

Carefully **cut open** one or more of the seeds you're using and draw a picture of what you see inside. If you're using more than one type of seed, make a note of what **similarities** and **differences** there are between them.

Do you think all seeds are the same **inside?** Why?

What would happen if you turned the jar **upside-down** after the seed started to grow?

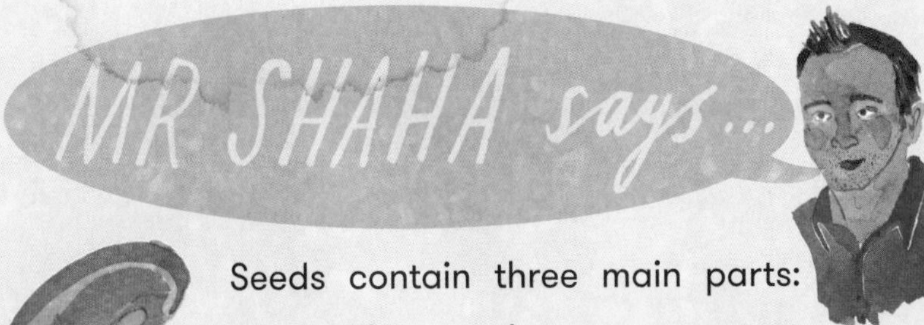
MR SHAHA says...

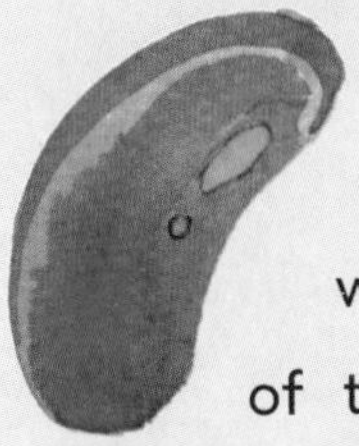

Seeds contain three main parts: a tough coating to protect what's inside, an embryo consisting of the root and shoot that will grow into the adult plant, and a store of food that allows the plant to grow before it can photosynthesise and start making its own food.

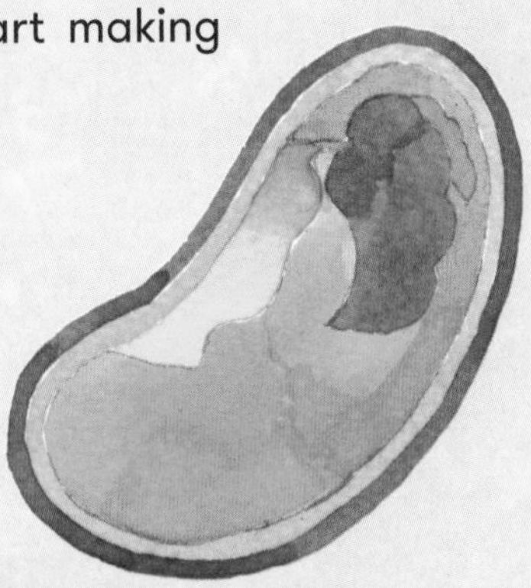

Germination is the process by which a seed begins to grow into a plant. To do this, it must have water, oxygen, a suitable temperature, and sometimes light. The precise conditions needed depend on the type of plant. Once these things are provided, the embryo can start growing and the embryonic root and shoot will break through the seed coating and form the roots and stem of a plant. Soon afterwards, the plant will produce leaves on the shoot and start making its own food through the process of photosynthesis.

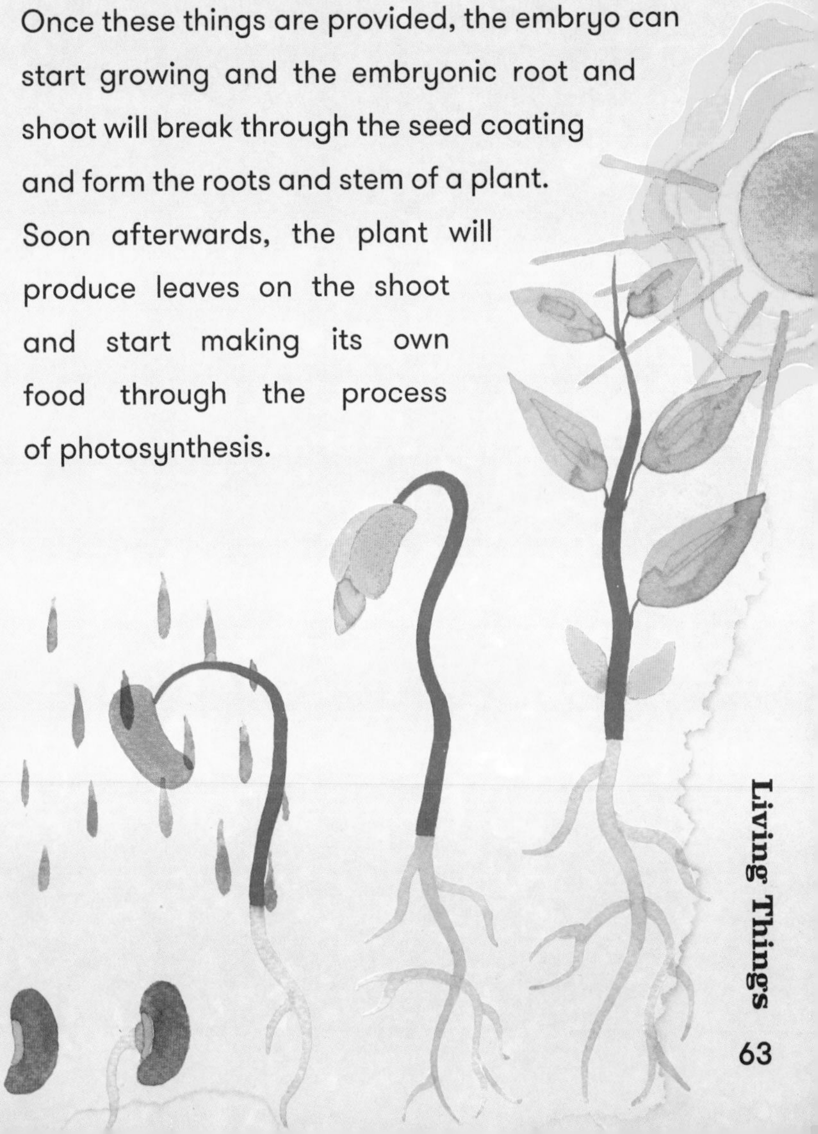

For Renu, Reuben, and Rafa
—A.S.

For my Mum, Karen Jane, who first revealed the wonder in drawing a line.
—E.R.

Acknowledgements

This book has been a real team effort and I'd first like to thank Emily Robertson for the gorgeous illustrations, which give it such a distinct look and feel.

I am endlessly grateful to my agent Catherine Clarke for her ongoing support and encouragement, and for taking me out for the lunch where we discussed cookery books and the idea for 'Recipes for Wonder' was born.

Thank you to the team at Scribe – Philip Gwyn Jones, Miriam Rosenbloom, Sarah Braybrooke, Kate O'Donnell, and Molly Slight – and designer Sarah Malley, for working so hard and taking such care to get the book right.

I first tried out many of the activities in this book while working at The Royal Institution and I owe a massive thank you to the team there for letting me have one of the most fun jobs of my career – Olympia Brown, Gail Cardew, Ed Prosser, Ant Lewis, Liina Hultgren, Cassie Williams, David Porter, Martin Davies and Andy Marmery. You can see the results of our work together at rigb.org/families/experimental.

There are lots of teachers and science communicators that I am indebted to, but I would like to say a special thanks to Paul McCrory and David Sang for encouraging me to write this book and for taking the time and trouble to check the science in it.

Jonathan Sanderson introduced me to the term 'wondersmith', but that's just one item on a very long list of things for which I owe him thanks.

Thank you to the staff and students at The Camden School for Girls and The Watford UTC for letting me be part of your communities.

Special thanks to Sarah Bearchall for the daffodil dissection activity, and Joe Wright for checking the biology activities.

Finally, thank you to Kate Fletcher, without whom my life would be far less filled with wonder.
—Alom

Alom, thank you for inviting me on this wondrous journey with you! You have opened my eyes once more to the delights that make up our world and it feels good.

Miri, Sarah and Philip thank you for your support, guidance and expert knowledge throughout this project. I am eternally grateful.

Katherine, Laurie and Michael my dear friends who gave their time and helpful thoughts, you guys are great.

Joseph - you are the positive to my negative, and the bringer of tea in the wee hours. I love you. Thank you.
—Emily

Published by Scribble, an imprint of Scribe Publications, 2018
18–20 Edward Street, Brunswick, Victoria 3056, Australia
2 John Street, Clerkenwell, London, WC1N 2ES, United Kingdom

Printed and bound in China by 1010
9781911344155 (UK hardback)
9781911344551 (UK paperback)
9781925321890 (Australian hardback)
CiP records for this title are available from the National Library of Australia and the British Library
scribblekidsbooks.com
scribepublications.com.au